"A wonderfully comprehensive book. The authors have made it easy to understand how our minds function and how to make changes so that we can live happier, fuller lives."
—Sharon Salzberg, author of *Lovingkindness*

"Solidly grounded in the latest neuroscientific research, and supported by a deep understanding of contemplative practice, this book is accessible, compelling, and profound—a crystallization of practical wisdom!"
—Philip David Zelazo, Ph.D., Nancy M. and John E. Lindahl Professor at the Institute of Child Development, University of Minnesota

"This is simply the best book I have r
shape our brains to be peaceful and
literally change your brain and your
—Jennifer Louden, author of *Th*
and *The Life Organizer*

"Buddha's Brain is a significant contribution to understanding the interface between science and meditation in the path of transformation. Illuminating."
—Joseph Goldstein, author of *A Heart Full of Peace* and *One Dharma*

"Buddha's Brain is compelling, easy to read, and quite educational. The book skillfully answers the central question of each of our lives—how to be happy—by presenting the core precepts of Buddhism integrated with a primer on how our brains function. This book will be helpful to anyone wanting to understand time-tested ways of skillful living backed up by up-to-date science."
—Frederic Luskin, Ph.D., author of *Forgive for Good* and director of Stanford Forgiveness Projects

"I wish I had a science teacher like Rick Hanson when I went to school. *Buddha's Brain* is at once fun, fascinating, and profound. It not only shows us effective ways to develop real happiness in our lives, but also explains physiologically how and why they work. As he instructs us to do with positive experiences, take in all the good information this book offers and savor it."

> —James Baraz, author of *Awakening Joy* and cofounder of Spirit Rock Meditation Center

"With the mind of a scientist, the perspective of a psychologist, and the wise heart of a parent and devoted meditator, Rick Hanson has created a guide for all of us who want to learn about and apply the scintillating new research that embraces neurology, psychology, and authentic spiritual inquiry. Up-to-date discoveries combined with state-of-the-art practices make this book an engaging read. *Buddha's Brain* is at the top of my list!"

> —Richard A. Heckler, Ph.D., assistant professor at John F. Kennedy University in Pleasant Hill, CA

"An illuminating guide to the emerging confluence of cutting-edge neuropsychology and ancient Buddhist wisdom filled with practical suggestions on how to gradually rewire your brain for greater happiness. Lucid, good-humored, and easily accessible."

> —John J. Prendergast, Ph.D., adjunct associate professor of psychology at California Institute of Integral Studies and senior editor of *The Sacred Mirror* and *Listening from the Heart of Silence*

"*Buddha's Brain* will show you how mental practices, informed by contemplative traditions, can increase your capacity for experiencing happiness and peace. This book provides a scientific understanding of these methods and clear guidance through practices that cultivate a wise and free heart."

> —Tara Brach, Ph.D. author of *Radical Acceptance*

"This book enables us to understand the whys and hows of our human operating system so we can make more informed actions that allow us to live our lives more fully, compassionately, and with greater well-being and kindness towards others and ourselves. What I find exciting about *Buddha's Brain* is Rick Hanson's ability to clearly delineate the root causes of suffering and explain pertinent ways we can actually change these causes and effect lasting change on all levels of our mind, body, and interpersonal relationships. His informative, relaxed, and easy-to-read style of writing made me want to pick up this book again and again and dive ever more deeply into the complexities of our human engineering. Buddha's Brain is now on my recommendation list for all my students and teachers-in-training."

— Richard C. Miller, Ph.D., founding president of
    Integrative Restoration Institute

"Numerous writings in recent years have exacerbated the traditional rift between science and religion; however, there has been a refreshing parallel movement in the opposite direction. Neuroscientists have become increasingly interested in using first-person introspective inquiries of the mind to complement their third-person, Western scientific investigations of the brain. Buddhist contemplative practices are particularly amenable to such collaboration, inviting efforts to find neurobiological explanations for Buddhist philosophy. Stripped of religious baggage, *Buddha's Brain* clearly describes how modern concepts of evolutionary and cognitive neurobiology support core Buddhist teachings and practice. This book should have great appeal for those seeking a secular spiritual path, while also raising many testable hypotheses for interested neuroscientists."

— Jerome Engel, Jr., MD, Ph.D., Jonathan Sinay
    Distinguished Professor of Neurology, Neurobiology, and
    Psychiatry and Biobehavioral Sciences at the University
    of California, Los Angeles

Buddha's Brain

the practical
neuroscience of
happiness, love
& wisdom

RICK HANSON, PH.D.
with RICHARD MENDIUS, MD

New Harbinger Publications, Inc.

Publisher's Note

Distributed in Canada by Raincoast Books

Copyright © 2009 by Rick Hanson
    New Harbinger Publications, Inc.
    5674 Shattuck Avenue
    Oakland, CA 94609
    www.newharbinger.com

Acquired by Melissa Kirk

FSC
www.fsc.org
MIX
Paper from responsible sources
FSC® C011935

Library of Congress Cataloging-in-Publication Data

Hanson, Rick.
  Buddha's brain : the practical neuroscience of happiness, love, and wisdom / Rick Hanson with Richard Mendius.
  p. cm.
  Includes bibliographical references.
  ISBN-13: 978-1-57224-695-9 (pbk. : alk. paper)
  ISBN-10: 1-57224-695-2 (pbk. : alk. paper) 1. Neuropsychology. 2. Happiness. 3. Love. 4. Wisdom. 5. Buddhism and science. I. Mendius, Richard. II. Title.
  QP360.H335 2009
  612.8--dc22

       2009023477

16 15 14

20 19 18 17 16 15 14 13

Contents

Part Four
Wisdom

Foreword

*B*uddha's Brain is an invitation to use the focus of your mind to harness the power of attention to enhance your life and your relationships with others. Synthesizing ancient insights from contemplative practice in the Buddhist traditions with modern discoveries from the field of neuroscience, Drs. Rick Hanson and Richard Mendius have assembled a thought-provoking and practical guide that walks you step-by-step through awakening your mind.

A revolution in science has recently revealed that the adult brain remains open to change throughout the lifespan. Though many brain scientists have in the past stated that the mind is just the activity of the brain, we now can look at the connection between these two dimensions of our lives from a different perspective. When we consider the mind as an embodied and relational process that regulates the flow of energy and information, we come to realize that we can actually use the mind to change the brain. The simple truth is that how we focus our attention, how we intentionally direct the flow of energy and information through our neural circuits, can directly alter the brain's activity and its structure. The key is to know the steps toward using our awareness in ways that promote well-being.

Knowing that the mind is relational and that the brain is the social organ of the body, we also come to another new point of view: Our relationships with one another are not a casual part of our lives; they are fundamental to how our minds function and are an essential aspect of brain health. Our social connections with one another shape our neural connections that form the structure of the brain. This means that the way we communicate alters the very circuitry of our brain, especially in ways that help keep our lives in balance. Science further verifies that when we cultivate compassion and mindful awareness in our lives—when we let go of judgments and attend fully to the present—we are harnessing the social circuits of the brain to enable us to transform even our relationship with our own self.

The authors have woven together Buddhist practices developed over two thousand years and new insights into the workings of the brain to offer us this guide to intentionally creating these positive changes in ourselves. Modern times often cause us to go on automatic pilot, continually multitasking and busying our lives with digital stimulation, information overload, and schedules that stress our brains and overwhelm our lives. Finding time to pause amidst this chaos has become an urgent need few of us take the time to satisfy. With *Buddha's Brain,* we are invited to take a deep breath and consider the neural reasons why we should slow ourselves down, balance our brain, and improve our connections with one another, and with our self.

The exercises offered here are based on practices that have been scientifically demonstrated to have positive effects in shaping our internal world by making us more focused, resilient, and resourceful. These well-established steps also enhance our empathy for others, widening our circles of compassion and care into the interconnected world in which we live. The promise of harnessing our minds to change our brains through these practices is to build the circuits of kindness and well-being moment by moment, one person, one relationship at a time. What more can we ask for? And what better time to begin than now?

Daniel J. Siegel, MD
Author, *Mindsight: The New Science of Personal Transformation* and *The Mindful Brain: Reflection and Attunement in the Cultivation of Well-Being*
Mindsight Institute and the UCLA Mindful Awareness Research Center
Los Angeles, California
June 2009

Preface

In *Buddha's Brain,* Drs. Rick Hanson and Richard Mendius offer you a beautifully clear and practical connection to the essential wisdom teachings of the Buddha. Using the contemporary language of scientific research, they invite the reader to open to the mysteries of the mind, bringing a modern understanding to the ancient and profound teachings of inner meditation practice. *Buddha's Brain* skillfully weaves these classical teachings with the revolutionary findings of neuroscience, which has begun to confirm the human capacities for mindfulness, compassion, and self-regulation that are central to contemplative training.

In reading this book, you will learn both brain science and practical inner ways to enhance well-being, develop ease and compassion, and reduce suffering. You will be introduced to wise new perspectives on life and the biological bases for fostering the development of this wisdom. These chapters will help you better understand the workings of the mind and the neurological roots of happiness, empathy, and interdependence.

The teachings that underlie each chapter—the noble truths, the foundations of mindfulness, and the development of virtue, loving-kindness, forgiveness, and inner peace—are straightforward and immediate, presented with the Buddha's openhanded invitation for each person to understand individually. The practices that follow these teachings are equally clear and authentic. They offer fundamentally the same trainings you would receive in a meditation temple.

I have seen Rick and Richard offer these teachings, and I respect how positively it affects the minds and hearts of those who come to practice with them.

More than ever, the human world needs to find ways to build love, understanding, and peace, individually and on a global scale.

May these words contribute to this critical endeavor.

Blessings,

Jack Kornfield, Ph.D.
Spirit Rock Center
Woodacre, California
June 2009

Acknowledgements

W e would like to thank and acknowledge many people:
Our spiritual teachers, including Christina Feldman,
James Baraz, Tara Brach, Ajahn Chah, Ajahn Amaro, Ajahn
Sumedho, Ajahn Brahm, Jack Kornfield, Sylvia Boorstein, Guy and
Sally Armstrong, Joseph Goldstein, Kamala Masters (special thanks
for the chapter on equanimity), Steve Armstrong, Gil Fronsdal,
Phillip Moffit, and Wes Nisker.

Our intellectual teachers and mentors, including Dan Siegel,
Evan Thompson, Richard Davidson, Mark Leary, Bernard Baars, Wil
Cunningham, Phil Zelazo, Antoine Lutz, Alan Wallace, William
Waldron, Andy Olendzki, Jerome Engel, Frank Benson, and Fred
Luskin; during the final preparation of this book, we came across a
paper written by Drs. Davidson and Lutz entitled "Buddha's Brain,"
and we respectfully acknowledge their prior use of that term; we
also bow to the memory of Francisco Varela.

Our benefactors, including Spirit Rock Meditation Center, the
Mind and Life Institute, Peter Bauman, the members of the San
Rafael Meditation Group, Patrick Anderson, Terry Patten, Daniel
Ellenberg, Judith Bell, Andy Dreitcer, Michael Hagerty, Julian Isaacs,
Stephen Levine, Richard Miller, Deanna Clark, the Community
Dharma Leaders Program, and Sue Thoele.

Our careful readers, who made many helpful suggestions,
including Linda Graham, Carolyn Pincus, Harold Hedelman, Steve
Meyers, Gay Watson, John Casey, Cheryl Wilfong, Jeremy Lent, and
John Prendergast.

Our wonderful editors and designers at New Harbinger, including Melissa Kirk, Jess Beebe, Amy Shoup, and Gloria Sturzenacker.

Our painstaking and large-hearted illustrator, Brad Reynolds (www.integralartandstudies.com).

Our families, including Jan, Forrest, and Laurel Hanson; Shelly Scammell; Courtney, Taryn, and Ian Mendius; William Hanson; Lynne and Jim Bramlett; Keith and Jenny Hanson; Patricia Winter Mendius, Catherine M. Graber, E. Louise Mendius, and Karen M. Chooljian.

And the many other people who have opened the mind and heart of each of us.

Introduction

This book is about how to reach inside your own brain to create more happiness, love, and wisdom. It explores the historically unprecedented intersection of psychology, neurology, and contemplative practice to answer two questions:

- What brain states underlie the mental states of happiness, love, and wisdom?

- How can you use your mind to stimulate and strengthen these positive brain states?

The result is a practical guide to your brain, full of tools you can use to gradually change it for the better.

Richard is a neurologist and I'm a neuropsychologist. While I've written most of the words here, Richard has been my long-time collaborator and teaching partner; his insights into the brain from his thirty years as a physician are woven into these pages. Together we've founded the Wellspring Institute for Neuroscience and Contemplative Wisdom; its website, www.wisebrain.org, offers many articles, talks, and other resources.

In this book you'll learn effective ways to deal with difficult states of mind, including stress, low mood, distractibility, relationship issues, anxiety, sorrow, and anger. But our main focus will be on positive well-being, psychological growth, and spiritual practice. For thousands of years, contemplatives—the Olympic athletes of mental training—have studied the mind. In this book we'll take the contemplative tradition we know best—Buddhism—and apply it to the brain to reveal neural pathways to happiness, love, and wisdom. No one knows the full nature of the brain of a Buddha or of any other person. But what is increasingly known is how to stimulate and strengthen the neural foundations of joyful, caring, and deeply insightful states of mind.

HOW TO USE THIS BOOK

You don't need any background in neuroscience, psychology, or meditation to use this book. It weaves together information and methods—like an operating manual for your brain combined with a toolbox—and you'll find the tools that work best for you.

Because the brain is fascinating, we've presented a good deal of the latest science about it, including numerous references in case you want to look up these studies yourself. (But to avoid this turning into a textbook, we've simplified the descriptions of neural activities to focus on their essential features.) On the other hand, if you're more interested in practical methods, it's fine to glide over the science parts. Of course, psychology and neurology are both such young sciences that there's a lot they don't understand yet. So we haven't attempted to be comprehensive. In fact, we've been opportunistic, focusing on methods that have a plausible scientific explanation for how they light up your neural networks of contentment, kindness, and peace.

These methods include some guided meditations. The instructions for these are deliberately loose, often including language that's poetic and evocative rather than narrow and specific. You can approach these in different ways: you might just read and think about them; you might bring parts of them into any meditative practices you are already doing; you might work through them with a friend; or you might record the instructions and do them by yourself. The instructions are just suggestions; pause as long as you like between them. There is no wrong way to do a meditation—the right way is what feels right to you.

A word of caution: This book isn't a substitute for professional care, and it is not a treatment for any mental or physical condition. Different things work for different people. Sometimes a method may stir up uncomfortable feelings, especially if you have a history of trauma. Feel free to ignore a method, discuss it with a friend (or counselor), change it, or drop it. Be kind to yourself.

Last, if I know one thing for sure, it's that you can do small things inside your mind that will lead to big changes in your brain and your experience of living. I've seen this happen again and again with people I've known as a psychologist or as a meditation teacher, and I've seen it in my own thoughts and feelings as well. You really can nudge your whole being in a better direction every day.

When you change your brain, you change your life.

chapter 1

The Self-Transforming Brain

The principal activities of brains are making changes in themselves.

—Marvin L. Minsky

W hen your mind changes, your brain changes, too. In the saying from the work of the psychologist Donald Hebb: when neurons fire together, they wire together—mental activity actually creates new neural structures (Hebb 1949; LeDoux 2003). As a result, even fleeting thoughts and feelings can leave lasting marks on your brain, much like a spring shower can leave little trails on a hillside.

For example, taxi drivers in London—whose job requires remembering lots of twisty streets—develop a larger hippocampus (a key brain region for making visual-spatial memories), since that part of the brain gets an extra workout (Maguire et al. 2000). As you become a happier person, the left frontal region of your brain becomes more active (Davidson 2004).

What flows through your mind sculpts your brain. Thus, *you can use your mind to change your brain for the better*—which will benefit your whole being, and every other person whose life you touch.

This book aims to show you how. You'll learn what the brain is doing when the mind is happy, loving, and wise. And you'll learn many ways to activate these brain states, strengthening them a bit each time. This will give you the ability to gradually rewire your own brain—from the inside out—for greater well-being, fulfillment in your relationships, and inner peace.

Your Brain—Basic Facts

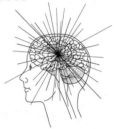

- Your brain is three pounds of tofu-like tissue containing 1.1 trillion cells, including 100 billion *neurons.* On average, each neuron receives about five thousand connections, called *synapses*, from other neurons (Linden 2007).

- At its receiving synapses, a neuron gets signals—usually as a burst of chemicals called *neurotransmitters*—from other neurons. Signals tell a neuron either to fire or not; whether it fires depends mainly on the combination of signals it receives each moment. In turn, when a neuron fires, it sends signals to other neurons through its transmitting synapses, telling them to fire or not.

- A typical neuron fires 5–50 times a second. In the time it takes you to read the bullet points in this box, literally quadrillions of signals will travel inside your head.

- Each neural signal is a bit of information; your nervous system moves information around like your heart moves blood around. All that information is what we define broadly as the *mind*, most of which is forever outside your awareness. In our use of the term, the "mind" includes the signals that regulate the stress response, the knowledge of how to ride a bike, personality tendencies, hopes and dreams, and the meaning of the words you're reading here.

- The brain is the primary mover and shaper of the mind. It's so busy that, even though it's only 2 percent of the body's weight, it uses 20–25 percent of its oxygen and glucose (Lammert 2008). Like a refrigerator, it's always humming away, performing its functions; consequently, it uses about the same amount of energy whether you're deep asleep or thinking hard (Raichle and Gusnard 2002).

- The number of possible combinations of 100 billion neurons firing or not is approximately 10 to the millionth power, or 1 followed by a million zeros, in principle; this is the number of possible states of your brain. To put this quantity in perspective, the number of atoms in the universe is estimated to be "only" about 10 to the eightieth power.

- Conscious mental events are based on temporary coalitions of synapses that form and disperse—usually within seconds—like eddies in a stream (Rabinovich, Huerta, and Laurent 2008). Neurons can also make lasting circuits, strengthening their connections to each other as a result of mental activity.

- The brain works as a whole system; thus, attributing some function—such as attention or emotion—to just one part of it is usually a simplification.

- Your brain interacts with other systems in your body—which in turn interact with the world—plus it's shaped by the mind as well. In the largest sense, your mind is made by your brain, body, natural world, and human culture—as well as by the mind itself (Thompson and Varela 2001). We're simplifying things when we refer to the brain as the basis of the mind.

- The mind and brain interact with each other so profoundly that they're best understood as a single, co-dependent, mind/ brain system.

AN UNPRECEDENTED OPPORTUNITY

Much as the microscope revolutionized biology, in the past few decades new research tools such as functional MRIs have led to a dramatic increase in scientific knowledge about the mind and brain. As a result, we now have many more ways to become happier and more effective in daily life.

Meanwhile, there's been a growing interest in the contemplative traditions, which have been investigating the mind—and thus the brain—for thousands of years, quieting the mind/brain enough to catch its softest murmurs and developing sophisticated ways to transform it. If you want to get good at anything, it helps to study those who have already mastered that skill, such as top chefs on TV if you like to cook. Therefore, if you'd like to feel more happiness, inner strength, clarity, and peace, it makes sense to learn from contemplative practitioners—both dedicated lay people and monastics—who've really pursued the cultivation of these qualities.

> We have probably learned more about the brain in the past twenty years than in all of recorded history.
> —Alan Leshner

Although "contemplative" may sound exotic, you've been contemplative if you've ever meditated, prayed, or just looked at the stars with a sense of wonder. The world has many contemplative traditions, most of which are associated with its major religions, including Christianity, Judaism, Islam, Hinduism, and Buddhism. Of these, science has engaged Buddhism the most. Like science, Buddhism encourages people to take nothing on faith alone and does not require a belief in God. It also has a detailed model of the mind that translates well to psychology and neurology. Consequently, with great respect for other contemplative traditions, we'll draw particularly on Buddhist perspectives and methods.

> Anything less than a contemplative perspective on life is an almost certain program for unhappiness.
> —Father Thomas Keating

Imagine each of these disciplines—psychology, neurology, and contemplative practice—as a circle (figure 1). The discoveries being made at that intersection are only just starting to show their promise, but scientists, clinicians, and contemplatives have already learned a great deal about the brain states that underlie wholesome mental states and

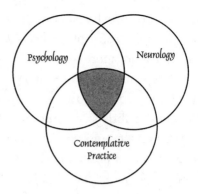

Figure 1
The Intersection of Three Disciplines

how to activate those brain states. These important discoveries give you a great ability to influence your own mind. You can use that ability to reduce any distress or dysfunction, increase well-being, and support spiritual practice; these are the central activities of what could be called the *path of awakening*, and our aim is to use brain science to help you travel far and well upon it. No book can give you the brain of a Buddha, but by better understanding the mind and brain of people who've gone a long way down this path, you can develop more of their joyful, caring, and insightful qualities within your own mind and brain as well.

> *The history of science is rich in the example of the fruitfulness of bringing two sets of techniques, two sets of ideas, developed in separate contexts for the pursuit of new truth, into touch with one another.*
> —J. Robert Oppenheimer

THE AWAKENING BRAIN

Richard and I both believe that something transcendental is involved with the mind, consciousness, and the path of awakening—call it God, Spirit, Buddha-nature, the Ground, or by no name at all. Whatever it is, by definition it's beyond the physical universe. Since it cannot be proven one way or another, it is important—and consistent with the spirit of science—to respect it as a possibility.

That said, more and more studies are showing how greatly the mind depends on the brain. For example, as the brain develops in childhood, so does the mind; if the brain is ever damaged, so is the mind. Subtle shifts in brain chemistry will alter mood, concentration, and memory (Meyer and Quenzer 2004). Using powerful magnets to suppress the emotion-processing limbic system changes how people make moral judgments (Knoch et al. 2006). Even some spiritual experiences correlate with neural activities (Vaitl et al. 2005).

Any aspect of the mind that is not transcendental must rely upon the physical processes of the brain. Mental activity, whether conscious or unconscious, maps to neural activity, much like a picture of a sunset on your computer screen maps to a pattern of magnetic charges on your hard drive. Apart from potential transcendental factors, the brain is the necessary and proximally sufficient condition for the mind; it's only *proximally* sufficient because the brain is nested in a larger network of biological and cultural causes and conditions, and is affected itself by the mind.

Of course, no one yet knows exactly *how* the brain makes the mind, or how—as Dan Siegel puts it—the mind uses the brain to make the mind. It's sometimes said that the greatest remaining scientific questions are: What caused the Big Bang? What is the grand unified theory that integrates quantum mechanics and general relativity? And what is the relationship between the mind and the brain, especially regarding conscious experience? The last question is up there with the other two because it is as difficult to answer, and as important.

To use an analogy, after Copernicus, most educated people accepted that the earth revolved around the sun. But no one knew how that actually happened. Roughly 150 years later, Isaac Newton developed the laws of gravity, which began to explain how the earth went about the sun. Then, after 200 more years, Einstein refined Newton's explanation through the theory of general relativity. It could be 350 years, and maybe longer, before we completely understand the relationship between the brain and the mind. But meanwhile, a reasonable working hypothesis is that *the mind is what the brain does.*

Therefore, an awakening mind means an awakening brain. Throughout history, unsung men and women and great teachers alike have cultivated remarkable mental states by generating remarkable brain states. For instance, when experienced Tibetan practitioners go deep into meditation, they produce uncommonly powerful and pervasive gamma *brainwaves* of electrical activity, in which unusually large regions of neural real estate pulse in synchrony 30–80 times a second (Lutz et al. 2004), integrating and unifying large territories of the mind. So, with a deep bow to the transcendental, we will stay within the frame of Western science and see what modern neuropsychology, informed by contemplative practice, offers in the way of effective methods for experiencing greater happiness, love, and wisdom.

To be sure: these methods will not replace traditional spiritual practices. You don't need an EEG or a Ph.D. in neuroscience to observe your experience and the world, and become a happier and kinder person. But understanding how to affect your own brain can be very helpful, especially for people who do not have time for intensive practice, such as the 24/7 grinding and polishing of monastic life.

THE CAUSES OF SUFFERING

Although life has many pleasures and joys, it also contains considerable discomfort and sorrow—the unfortunate side effect of three strategies that evolved to help animals, including us, pass on their genes. For sheer survival, these strategies work great, but they also lead to suffering (as we'll explore in depth in the two next chapters). To summarize, whenever a strategy runs into trouble, uncomfortable—sometimes even agonizing—alarm signals pulse through the nervous system to set the animal back on track. But trouble comes all the time, since each strategy contains inherent contradictions, as the animal tries to:

- Separate what is actually connected, in order to create a boundary between itself and the world

- Stabilize what keeps changing, in order to maintain its internal systems within tight ranges

- Hold onto fleeting pleasures and escape inevitable pains, in order to approach opportunities and avoid threats

Most animals don't have nervous systems complex enough to allow these strategies' alarms to grow into significant distress. But our vastly more developed brain is fertile ground for a harvest of suffering. Only we humans worry about the future, regret the past, and blame ourselves for the present. We get frustrated when we can't have what we want, and disappointed when what we like ends. We suffer *that* we suffer. We get upset about being in pain, angry about dying, sad about waking up sad yet another day. This kind of suffering—which encompasses most of our unhappiness and dissatisfaction—is constructed by the brain. It is made up. Which is ironic, poignant—and supremely hopeful.

For if the brain is the cause of suffering, it can also be its cure.

VIRTUE, MINDFULNESS, AND WISDOM

More than two thousand years ago, a young man named Siddhartha—not yet enlightened, not yet called the Buddha—spent many years training his mind and thus his brain. On the night of his awakening, he looked deep inside his mind (which reflected and revealed the underlying activities of his brain) and saw there both the causes of suffering and the path to freedom from suffering. Then, for forty years, he wandered northern India, teaching all who would listen how to:

- Cool the fires of greed and hatred to live with integrity

- Steady and concentrate the mind to see through its confusions

- Develop liberating insight

In short, he taught virtue, mindfulness (also called concentration), and wisdom. These are the three pillars of Buddhist practice, as well as the wellsprings of everyday well-being, psychological growth, and spiritual realization.

Virtue simply involves regulating your actions, words, and thoughts to create benefits rather than harms for yourself and others. In your brain, virtue draws on top-down direction from the *prefrontal cortex* (PFC); "prefrontal" means the most forward parts of the brain, just behind and above the forehead, and your "cortex" is the outer layer of the brain (its Latin root means "bark"). Virtue also relies on bottom-up calming from the *parasympathetic* nervous system and positive emotions from the *limbic* system. You'll learn how to work with the circuitry of these systems in chapter 5. Further on, we'll explore virtue in relationships, since that's where it's often most challenged, and then build on that foundation to nurture the brain states of empathy, kindness, and love (see chapters 8, 9, and 10).

Mindfulness involves the skillful use of attention to both your inner and outer worlds. Since your brain learns mainly from what you attend to, mindfulness is the doorway to taking in good experiences and making them a part of yourself (we'll discuss how to do this in chapter 4). We'll explore ways to activate the brain states that promote mindfulness, including to the point of deep meditative absorption, in chapters 11 and 12.

Wisdom is applied common sense, which you acquire in two steps. First, you come to understand what hurts and what helps—in other words, the causes of suffering and the path to its end (the focus of chapters 2 and 3). Then, based on this understanding, you let go of those things that hurt and strengthen those that help (chapters 6 and 7). As a result, over time you'll feel more connected with everything, more serene about how all things change and end, and more able to meet pleasure and pain without grasping after the one and struggling with the other. Finally, chapter 13 addresses what is perhaps the most seductive and subtle challenge to wisdom: the sense of being a self who is separate from and vulnerable to the world.

Regulation, Learning, and Selection

Virtue, mindfulness, and wisdom are supported by the three fundamental functions of the brain: regulation, learning, and selection. Your brain regulates itself—and other bodily systems—through a combination of excitatory and inhibitory activity: green lights and red lights. It learns through forming new circuits and strengthening or weakening existing ones. And it selects whatever experience has taught it to value; for example, even an earthworm can be trained to pick a particular path to avoid an electric shock.

These three functions—regulation, learning, and selection—operate at all levels of the nervous system, from the intricate molecular dance at the tip of a synapse to the whole-brain integration of control, competence, and discernment. All three functions are involved in any important mental activity.

Nonetheless, each pillar of practice corresponds quite closely to one of the three fundamental neural functions. Virtue relies heavily on regulation, both to excite positive inclinations and to inhibit negative ones. Mindfulness leads to new learning—since attention shapes neural circuits—and draws upon past learning to develop a steadier and more concentrated awareness. Wisdom is a matter of making choices, such as letting go of lesser pleasures for the sake of greater ones. Consequently, developing virtue, mindfulness, and wisdom in your mind depends on improving regulation, learning, and selection in your brain. Strengthening the three neural functions—which you'll learn to do in the pages ahead—thus buttresses the pillars of practice.

INCLINING THE MIND

When you set out on the path of awakening, you begin wherever you are. Then—with time, effort, and skillful means—virtue, mindfulness, and wisdom gradually strengthen and you feel happier and more loving. Some traditions describe this process as an uncovering of the true nature that was always present; others frame it as a transformation of your mind and body. Of course, these two aspects of the path of awakening support each other.

On the one hand, your true nature is both a refuge and a resource for the sometimes difficult work of psychological growth and spiritual practice. It's a remarkable fact that the people who have gone the very deepest into the mind—the sages and saints of every religious tradition—all say essentially the same thing: your fundamental nature is pure, conscious, peaceful, radiant, loving, and wise, and it is joined in mysterious ways with the ultimate underpinnings of reality, by whatever name we give That. Although your true nature may be hidden momentarily by stress and worry, anger and unfulfilled longings, it still continues to exist. Knowing this can be a great comfort.

On the other hand, working with the mind and body to encourage the development of what's wholesome—and the uprooting of what's not—is central to every path of psychological and spiritual development. Even if practice is a matter of "removing the obscurations" to true nature—to borrow a phrase from Tibetan Buddhism—the clearing of these is a progressive process of training, purification, and transformation. Paradoxically, it takes time to become what we already are.

In either case, these changes in the mind—uncovering inherent purity and cultivating wholesome qualities—reflect changes in the brain. By understanding better how the brain works and changes—how it gets emotionally hijacked or settles into calm virtue; how it creates distractibility or fosters mindful attention; how it makes harmful choices or wise ones—you can take more control of your brain, and therefore your mind. This will make your development of greater well-being, lovingness, and insight easier and more fruitful, and help you go as far as you possibly can on your own path of awakening.

BEING ON YOUR OWN SIDE

It's a general moral principle that the more power you have over someone, the greater your duty is to use that power benevolently. Well, who is the one person in the world you have the greatest power over? It's your future self. You hold that life in your hands, and what it will be depends on how you care for it.

One of the central experiences of my life occurred one evening around Thanksgiving, when I was about six years old. I remember standing across the street from our house, on the edge of cornfields in Illinois, seeing ruts in the dark soil filled with water from a recent rain. On the distant hills, tiny lights twinkled. I felt quiet and clear inside, and sad about the unhappiness that night in my home. Then it came to me very powerfully: it was up to *me*, and no one else, to find my way over time toward those faraway lights and the possibility of happiness they represented.

That moment has stayed with me because of what it taught me about what is and isn't within our control. It's impossible to change the past or the present: you can only accept all that as it is. But you *can* tend to the causes of a better future. Most of the ways you'll do this are small and humble. To use examples from later in this book, you could take a very full inhalation in a tense meeting to force a long exhalation, thus activating the calming parasympathetic nervous system (PNS). Or, when remembering an upsetting experience, recall the feeling of being with someone who loves you—which will gradually infuse the upsetting memory with a positive feeling. Or, to steady the mind, deliberately prolong feelings of happiness as this will increase levels of the neurotransmitter dopamine, which will help your attention stay focused.

These little actions really add up over time. Every day, ordinary activities—as well as any personal growth or spiritual practices—contain dozens of opportunities to change your brain from the inside out. You really do have that power, which is a wonderful thing in a world full of forces beyond your control. A single raindrop doesn't have much effect, but if you have enough raindrops and enough time, you can carve a Grand Canyon.

But to take these steps, you have to be on your own side. That may not be so easy at first; most people bring less kindness to themselves than to others. To get on your own side, it can be helpful to make a convincing case for tending to the causes that will change your brain for the better. For example, please consider these facts:

- You were once a young child, just as worthy of care as any other. Can you see yourself as a child? Wouldn't you wish the best for that little person? The same is true today: you are a human being like any other—and just as deserving of happiness, love, and wisdom.

- Progressing along your path of awakening will make you more effective in your work and relationships. Think about the many ways that others will benefit from you being more good-humored, warm-hearted, and savvy. Nurturing your own development isn't selfish. It's actually a great gift to other people.

THE WORLD ON THE EDGE OF A SWORD

Perhaps most important of all, consider the ripples spreading out from your own growth, imperceptibly but genuinely helping a world full of greed, confusion, fear, and anger. Our world is poised on the edge of a sword, and it could tip either way. Across the planet, slowly but surely, we're seeing increasing democratization, a growing number of grassroots organizations, and more understanding of our fragile interconnectedness. On the other hand, the world is getting hotter, military technologies are increasingly lethal, and a billion people go to sleep hungry every night.

The tragedy and the opportunity of this moment in history are exactly the same: the natural and technical resources needed to pull us back from the brink *already exist*. The issue is not a lack of resources. It is a lack of will and restraint, of attention to what's truly happening, and of enlightened self-interest—a shortage, in other words, of virtue, mindfulness, and wisdom.

As you and other people become increasingly skillful with the mind—and thus the brain—that could help tip our world in a better direction.

---

chapter 1: KEY POINTS

֍ What happens in your mind changes your brain, both temporarily and in lasting ways; neurons that fire together wire together. And what happens in your brain changes your mind, since the brain and mind are a single, integrated system.

֍ Therefore, you can use your mind to change your brain to benefit your mind—and everyone else whose life you touch.

֍ People who have practiced deeply in the contemplative traditions are the "Olympic athletes" of the mind. Learning how they've trained their minds (and thus their brains) reveals powerful ways to have more happiness, love, and wisdom.

֍ The brain evolved to help you survive, but its three primary survival strategies also make you suffer.

֍ Virtue, mindfulness, and wisdom are the pillars of everyday well-being, personal growth, and spiritual practice; they draw on the three fundamental neural functions of regulation, learning, and selection.

❀ The path of awakening involves both transforming the mind/brain and uncovering the wonderful true nature that was there all along.

❀ Small positive actions every day will add up to large changes over time, as you gradually build new neural structures. To keep at it, you need to be on your own side.

❀ Wholesome changes in the brains of many people could help tip the world in a better direction.

Part One

The Causes of
Suffering

chapter 2

The Evolution of Suffering

Nothing in biology makes sense except in light of evolution.
—Theodosius Dobzhansky

There's a lot about life that's wonderful, but it has its hard parts, too. Look at the faces around you—they probably hold a fair amount of strain, disappointment, and worry. And you know your own frustrations and sorrows as well. The pangs of living range from subtle loneliness and dismay, to moderate stress, hurt, and anger, and then to intense trauma and anguish. This whole range is what we mean by the word, *suffering*. A lot of suffering is mild but chronic, such as a background sense of anxiety, irritability, or lack of fulfillment. It's natural to want less of this. And in its place, more contentment, love, and peace.

To make any problem better, you need to understand its causes. That's why all the great physicians, psychologists, and spiritual teachers have been master diagnosticians. For example, in his Four Noble Truths, the Buddha identified an ailment (suffering), diagnosed its cause (craving: a compelling sense of need for something), specified its cure (freedom from craving), and prescribed a treatment (the Eightfold Path).

This chapter examines suffering in light of evolution in order to diagnose its sources in your brain. When you understand *why* you feel nervous, annoyed, hassled, driven, blue, or inadequate, those feelings have less power over you. This by itself can bring some relief. Your understanding will also help you make better use of the "prescriptions" in the rest of this book.

The Evolving Brain

- Life began around 3.5 billion years ago. Multicelled creatures first appeared about 650 million years ago. (When you get a cold, remember that microbes had nearly a three-billion-year head-start!) By the time the earliest jellyfish arose about 600 million years ago, animals had grown complex enough that their sensory and motor systems needed to communicate with each other; thus the beginnings of neural tissue. As animals evolved, so did their nervous systems, which slowly developed a central headquarters in the form of a brain.

- Evolution builds on preexisting capabilities. Life's progression can be seen inside your own brain, in terms of what Paul MacLean (1990) referred to as the reptilian, paleomammalian, and neo-mammalian levels of development (see figure 2; all figures are somewhat inexact and for illustrative purposes only).

- Cortical tissues that are relatively recent, complex, conceptualizing, slow, and motivationally diffuse sit atop *subcortical* and *brain-stem* structures that are ancient, simplistic, concrete, fast, and motivationally intense. (The subcortical region lies in the center of your brain, beneath the cortex and on top of the brain stem; the brain stem roughly corresponds to the "reptilian brain" seen in figure 2.) As you go through your day, there's a kind of lizard-squirrel-monkey brain in your head shaping your reactions from the bottom up.

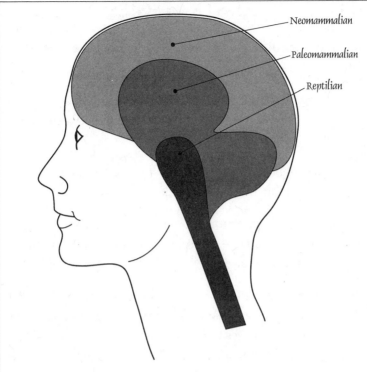

Figure 2
The Evolving Brain

- Nonetheless, the modern cortex has great influence over the rest of the brain, and it's been shaped by evolutionary pressures to develop ever-improving abilities to parent, bond, communicate, cooperate, and love (Dunbar and Shultz 2007).

- The cortex is divided into two "hemispheres" connected by the *corpus callosum*. As we evolved, the left hemisphere (in most people) came to focus on sequential and linguistic processing while the right hemisphere specialized in holistic and visual-spatial processing; of course, the two halves of your brain work closely together. Many neural structures are duplicated so that there is one in each hemisphere; nonetheless, the usual convention is to refer to a structure in the singular (e.g., the hippocampus).

THREE SURVIVAL STRATEGIES

Over hundreds of millions of years of evolution, our ancestors developed three fundamental strategies for survival:

- Creating separations—in order to form boundaries between themselves and the world, and between one mental state and another

- Maintaining stability—in order to keep physical and mental systems in a healthy balance

- Approaching opportunities and avoiding threats—in order to gain things that promote offspring, and escape or resist things that don't

These strategies have been extraordinarily effective for survival. But Mother Nature doesn't care how they *feel*. To motivate animals, including ourselves, to follow these strategies and pass on their genes, neural networks evolved to create pain and distress under certain conditions: when separations break down, stability is shaken, opportunities disappoint, and threats loom. Unfortunately, these conditions happen all the time, because:

- Everything is connected.

- Everything keeps changing.

- Opportunities routinely remain unfulfilled or lose their luster, and many threats are inescapable (e.g., aging and death)

Let's see how all this makes you suffer.

NOT SO SEPARATE

The parietal *lobes* of the brain are located in the upper back of the head (a "lobe" is a rounded swelling of the cortex). For most people, the left lobe establishes that the body is distinct from the world, and the right lobe indicates where the body is compared to features in its environment. The result is an automatic, underlying assumption along the lines of *I am separate and independent.* Although this is true in some ways, in many important ways it is not.

Not So Distinct

To live, an organism must *metabolize*: it must exchange matter and energy with its environment. Consequently, over the course of a year, many of the atoms in your body are replaced by new ones. The energy you use to get a drink of water comes from sunshine working its way up to you through the food chain—in a real sense, light lifts the cup to your lips. The apparent wall between your body and the world is more like a picket fence.

And between your mind and the world, it's like a line painted on the sidewalk. Language and culture enter and pattern your mind from the moment of birth (Han and Northoff 2008). Empathy and love naturally attune you to other people, so your mind moves into resonance with theirs (Siegel 2007). These flows of mental activity go both ways as you influence others.

Within your mind, there are hardly any lines at all. All its contents flow into each other, sensations becoming thoughts feelings desires actions and more sensations. This stream of consciousness correlates with a cascade of fleeting neural assemblies, each assembly dispersing into the next one, often in less than a second (Dehaene, Sergent, and Changeux 2003; Thompson and Varela 2001).

Not So Independent

I'm here because a Serbian nationalist assassinated Archduke Ferdinand, catalyzing World War I—which in turn led to the unlikely meeting of my mom and dad at an Army dance in 1944. Of course, there are ten thousand reasons why *anyone* is here today. How far back should we go? My son—born with his umbilical cord wrapped around his neck—is here due to medical technologies developed over hundreds of years.

Or we could go *way* back: Most of the atoms in your body—including the oxygen in your lungs and the iron in your blood—were born inside a star. In the early universe, hydrogen was just about the only element. Stars are giant fusion reactors that pound together hydrogen atoms, making heavier elements and releasing lots of energy in the process. The ones that went nova spewed their contents far and wide. By the time our solar system started to form, roughly nine billion years after the universe began, enough large atoms existed to make our planet, to make the hands that hold this book and the brain that understands these words. Truly, you're here because a lot of stars blew up. Your body is made of stardust.

Your mind also depends on countless preceding causes. Think of the life events and people that have shaped your views, personality, and emotions. Imagine having been switched at birth and raised by poor shopkeepers in Kenya or a wealthy oil family in Texas; how different would your mind be today?

The Suffering of Separation

Since we are each connected and interdependent with the world, our attempts to be separate and independent are regularly frustrated, which produces painful signals of disturbance and threat. Further, even when our efforts are temporarily successful, they still lead to suffering. When you regard the world as "not me at all," it is potentially unsafe, leading you to fear and resist it. Once you say, "I am *this* body apart from the world," the body's frailties become your own. If you think it weighs too much or doesn't look right, you suffer. If it's threatened by illness, aging, and death—as all bodies are—you suffer.

NOT SO PERMANENT

Your body, brain, and mind contain vast numbers of systems that must maintain a healthy equilibrium. The problem, though, is that changing conditions continually disturb these systems, resulting in signals of threat, pain, and distress—in a word, suffering.

We Are Dynamically Changing Systems

Let's consider a single neuron, one that releases the neurotransmitter serotonin (see figures 3 and 4). This tiny neuron is both part of the nervous system and a complex system in its own right that requires multiple subsystems to keep it running. When it fires, tendrils at the end of its axon expel a burst of molecules into the synapses—the connections—it makes with other neurons. Each tendril contains about two hundred little bubbles called *vesicles* that are full of the neurotransmitter serotonin (Robinson 2007). Every time the neuron fires, five to ten vesicles spill open. Since a typical neuron fires around ten times a second, the serotonin vesicles of each tendril are emptied out every few seconds.

Consequently, busy little molecular machines must either manufacture new serotonin or recycle loose serotonin floating around the neuron. Then they need to build vesicles, fill them with serotonin, and move them close to where the action is, at the tip of each tendril. That's a lot of processes to keep in balance, with many things that could go wrong—and serotonin metabolism is just one of the thousands of systems in your body.

A Typical Neuron

- Neurons are the basic building blocks of the nervous system; their main function is to communicate with each other across tiny junctions called synapses. While there are many sorts of neurons, their basic design is pretty similar.

- The cell body sends out spikes called *dendrites* which receive neurotransmitters from other neurons. (Some neurons communicate directly with each other through electrical impulses.)

- Simplifying some, the millisecond-by-millisecond sum of all the excitatory and inhibitory signals a neuron receives determines whether or not it will fire.

- When a neuron fires, an electrochemical wave ripples down its *axon*, the fiber extending toward the neurons it sends signals to. This releases neurotransmitters into its synapses with receiving neurons, either inhibiting them or exciting them to fire in turn.

- Nerve signals are sped up by *myelin*, a fatty substance that insulates axons.

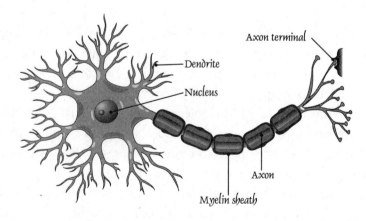

Figure 3
A (simplified) Neuron

• The gray matter of your brain is composed largely of the cell bodies of neurons. There is also white matter, made up of the axons and the *glial* cells; glial cells perform metabolic support functions such as wrapping axons in myelin and recycling neurotransmitters. Neuronal cell bodies are like 100 billion on-off switches connected by their axonal "wires" in an intricate network inside your head.

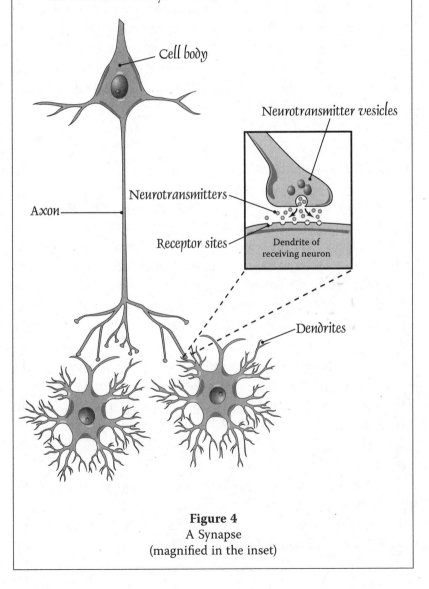

Figure 4
A Synapse
(magnified in the inset)

The Challenges of Maintaining an Equilibrium

For you to stay healthy, each system in your body and mind must balance two conflicting needs. On the one hand, it must remain open to inputs during ongoing transactions with its local environment (Thompson 2007); closed systems are dead systems. On the other hand, each system must also preserve a fundamental stability, staying centered around a good set-point and within certain ranges—not too hot, nor too cold. For example, inhibition from the prefrontal cortex (PFC) and arousal from the limbic system must balance each other: too much inhibition and you feel numb inside, too much arousal and you feel overwhelmed.

Signals of Threat

To keep each of your systems in balance, sensors register its state (as the thermometer does inside a thermostat) and send signals to regulators to restore equilibrium if the system gets out of range (i.e., turn the furnace on or off). Most of this regulation stays out of your awareness. But some signals for corrective action are so important that they bubble up into consciousness. For example, if your body gets too cold, you feel chilled; if it gets too hot, you feel like you're baking.

These consciously experienced signals are unpleasant, in part because they carry a sense of threat—a call to restore equilibrium before things slide too far too fast down the slippery slope. The call may come softly, with a sense of unease, or loudly, with alarm, even panic. However it comes, it mobilizes your brain to do whatever it takes to get you back in balance.

This mobilization usually comes with feelings of craving; these range from quiet longings to a desperate sense of compulsion. It is interesting that the word for craving in Pali—the language of early Buddhism—is *tanha*, the root of which means thirst. The word "thirst" conveys the visceral power of threat signals, even when they have nothing to do with life or limb, such as the possibility of being rejected. Threat signals are effective precisely because they're unpleasant—because they make you suffer, sometimes a little, sometimes a lot. You want them to stop.

Everything Keeps Changing

Occasionally, threat signals do stop for a while—just as long as every system stays in balance. But since the world is always changing, there are endless disturbances in the equilibria of your body, mind, and relationships. The regulators of the systems of your life, from the molecular bottom all the way up to the interpersonal top, must keep trying to impose static order on inherently unstable processes.

Consider the impermanence of the physical world, from the volatility of quantum particles to our own Sun, which will someday swell into a red giant and swallow the Earth. Or consider the turbulence of your nervous system; for example, regions in the PFC that support consciousness are updated five to eight times a second (Cunningham and Zelazo 2007).

This neurological instability underlies all states of mind. For example, every thought involves a momentary partitioning of streaming neural traffic into a coherent assembly of synapses that must soon disperse into fertile disorder to allow other thoughts to emerge (Atmanspacher and Graben 2007). Observe even a single breath, and you will experience its sensations changing, dispersing, and disappearing soon after they arise.

Everything changes. That's the universal nature of outer reality and inner experience. Therefore, there's no end to disturbed equilibria as long as you live. But to help you survive, your brain keeps trying to stop the river, struggling to hold dynamic systems in place, to find fixed patterns in this variable world, and to construct permanent plans for changing conditions. Consequently, your brain is forever chasing after the moment that has just passed, trying to understand and control it.

It's as if we live at the edge of a waterfall, with each moment rushing at us—experienced only and always *now* at the lip—and then zip, it's over the edge and gone. But the brain is forever clutching at what has just surged by.

NOT SO PLEASANT OR PAINFUL

In order to pass on their genes, our animal ancestors had to choose correctly many times a day whether to approach something or avoid it. Today, humans approach and avoid mental states as well as physical objects; for example, we pursue self-worth and push away shame. Nonetheless, for all its sophistication, human approaching and avoiding draws on much the same neural circuitry used by a monkey to look for bananas or a lizard to hide under a rock.

The Feeling Tone of Experience

How does your brain decide if something should be approached or avoided? Let's say you're walking in the woods; you round a bend and suddenly see a curvy shape on the ground right smack in front of you. To simplify a complex process, during the first few tenths of a second, light bouncing off this curved object is sent to the *occipital* cortex (which handles visual information) for processing into a meaningful image (see figure 5). Then the occipital cortex sends representations of this image in two directions: to the hippocampus, for evaluation as a potential threat or opportunity, and to the PFC and other parts of the brain for more sophisticated—and time-consuming—analysis.

Just in case, your hippocampus immediately compares the image to its short list of jump-first-think-later dangers. It quickly

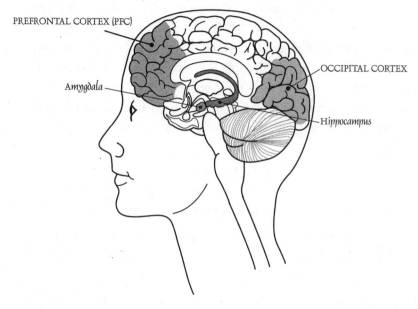

Figure 5
You See a Potential Threat or Opportunity

finds curvy shapes on its danger list, causing it to send a high-priority alert to your *amygdala*: "Watch out!" The amygdala—which is like an alarm bell—then pulses both a general warning throughout your brain and a special fast-track signal to your fight-or-flight neural and hormonal systems (Rasia-Filho, Londero, and Achaval 2000). We'll explore the details of the fight-or-flight cascade in the next chapter; the point here is that a second or so after you spot the curving shape, you jump back in alarm.

Meanwhile, the powerful but relatively slow PFC has been pulling information out of long-term memory to figure out whether the darn thing is a snake or a stick. As a few more seconds tick by, the PFC zeros in on the object's inert nature—and the fact that several people ahead of you walked past it without saying anything—and concludes that it's only a stick.

Throughout this episode, everything you experienced was either pleasant, unpleasant, or neutral. At first there were neutral or pleasant sights as you strolled along the path, then unpleasant fear at a potential snake, and finally pleasant relief at the realization that it was just a stick. That aspect of experience—whether it is pleasant, unpleasant, or neutral—is called, in Buddhism, its *feeling tone* (or, in Western psychology, its *hedonic tone*). The feeling tone is produced mainly by your amygdala (LeDoux 1995) and then broadcast widely. It's a simple but effective way to tell your brain as a whole what to do each moment: approach pleasant carrots, avoid unpleasant sticks, and move on from anything else.

Key Neurochemicals

These are the major chemicals inside your brain that affect neural activity; they have many functions, and we've listed here the ones that are relevant to this book.

Primary Neurotransmitters

- Glutamate—excites receiving neurons.

- GABA—inhibits receiving neurons.

Neuromodulators

These substances—sometimes also called neurotransmitters—influence the primary neurotransmitters. Because they're released widely within the brain, they have a powerful effect.

- Serotonin—regulates mood, sleep, and digestion; most antidepressants aim at increasing its effects.

- Dopamine—involved with rewards and attention; promotes approach behaviors.

- Norepinephrine—alerts and arouses.

- Acetylcholine—promotes wakefulness and learning.

Neuropeptides

These neuromodulators are built from *peptides,* a particular kind of organic molecule.

- Opioids—buffer stress, provide soothing and reduce pain, and produce pleasure (e.g., runner's high); these include endorphins.

- Oxytocin—promotes nurturing behaviors toward children and bonding in couples; associated with blissful closeness and love; women have more oxytocin than men.

- Vasopressin—supports pair bonding; in men it may promote aggressiveness toward sexual rivals.

Other Neurochemicals

- Cortisol—released by the adrenal glands during the stress response; stimulates the amygdala and inhibits the hippocampus.

- Estrogen—the brains of both men and women contain estrogen receptors; affects libido, mood, and memory.

Chasing Carrots

Two major neural systems keep you chasing carrots. The first system is based on the neurotransmitter dopamine. Dopamine-releasing neurons become more active when you encounter things that are linked to rewards in the past—for example, if you get a message from a good friend you haven't seen for a few months. These neurons also rev up when you encounter something that could offer rewards in the future—such as your friend saying she wants to take you to lunch. In your mind, this neural activity produces a motivating sense of desire: you want to call her back. When you do have lunch, a part of your brain called the *cingulate cortex* (about the size of your finger, on the interior edge of each hemisphere) tracks whether the rewards you expected—fun with your friend, good food—actually arrive (Eisenberger and Lieberman 2004). If they do, dopamine levels stay steady. But if you're disappointed—maybe your friend is in a bad mood—the cingulate sends out a signal that lowers dopamine levels. Falling dopamine registers in subjective experience as an unpleasant feeling tone—a dissatisfaction and discontent—that stimulates craving (broadly defined) for something that will restore its levels.

The second system, based on several other neuromodulators, is the biochemical source of the pleasant feeling tones that come from the actual—and anticipated—carrots in life. When these "pleasure chemicals"—natural opioids (including endorphins), oxytocin, and norepinephrine—surge into your synapses, they strengthen the neural circuits that are active, making them more likely to fire together in the future. Imagine a toddler trying to eat a spoonful of pudding. After many misses, his perceptual-motor neurons finally get it right, leading to waves of pleasure chemicals which help cement the synaptic connections that created the specific movements that slipped the spoon into his mouth.

In essence, this pleasure system highlights whatever triggered it, prompts you to pursue those rewards again, and strengthens the behaviors that make you successful in getting them. It works hand in hand with the dopamine-based system. For example, slaking your thirst feels good both because the discontent of low dopamine leaves, and because the pleasure chemical–based joy of cool water on a hot day arrives.

Approaching Involves Suffering

These two neural systems are necessary for survival. Additionally, you can use them for positive aims that have nothing to do with passing on genes. For example, you could increase your motivation to keep doing something healthy (e.g., exercise) by being really mindful of its rewards, such as feelings of vitality and strength.

But reaching for what's pleasant can also make you suffer:

- Desiring itself can be an unpleasant experience; even mild longing is subtly uncomfortable.

- When you can't have things you desire, it's natural to feel frustrated, disappointed, and discouraged—perhaps even hopeless and despairing.

- When you do fulfill a desire, the rewards that follow are often not that great. They're okay, but look closely at your experience: Is the cookie really that tasty—especially after the third bite? Was the satisfaction of the good job review that intense or long lasting?

- When rewards are in fact pretty great, many of them still come at a stiff price—big desserts are an obvious example. Also consider the rewards of gaining recognition, winning an argument, or getting others to act a particular way. What is the cost/benefit ratio, *really*?

- Even if you do get what you want, it's genuinely great, and it doesn't cost much—the gold standard—every pleasant experience must inevitably change and end. Even the best ones of all. You are routinely separated from things you enjoy. And someday that separation will be permanent. Friends drift away, children leave home, careers end, and eventually your own final breath comes and goes. Everything that begins must also cease. Everything that comes together must also disperse. Experiences are thus incapable of being completely satisfying. They are an unreliable basis for true happiness.

To use an analogy from the Thai meditation master Ajahn Chah: if getting upset about something unpleasant is like being bitten by a snake, grasping for what's pleasant is like grabbing the snake's tail; sooner or later, it will still bite you.

Sticks Are Stronger than Carrots

So far, we've discussed carrots and sticks as if they were equals. But actually, sticks are usually more powerful, since your brain is built more for avoiding than for approaching. That's because it's the negative experiences, not the positive ones, that have generally had the most impact on survival.

For example, imagine our mammalian ancestors dodging dinosaurs in a worldwide Jurassic Park 70 million years ago. Constantly looking over their shoulders, alert to the slightest crackle of brush, ready to freeze or bolt or attack depending on the situation. The quick and the dead. If they missed out on a carrot—a chance at food or mating, perhaps—they usually had other opportunities later. But if they failed to duck a stick—like a predator—then they'd probably be killed, with no chance at any carrots in the future. The ones that lived to pass on their genes paid a *lot* of attention to negative experiences.

Let's explore six ways your brain keeps you dodging sticks.

VIGILANCE AND ANXIETY

When you're awake and not doing anything in particular, the baseline resting state of your brain activates a "default network," and one of its functions seems to be tracking your environment and body for possible threats (Raichle et al. 2001). This basic awareness is often accompanied by a background feeling of anxiety that keeps you vigilant. Try walking through a store for a few minutes without the least whiff of caution, unease, or tension. It's very difficult.

This makes sense because our mammalian, primate, and human ancestors were prey as well as predators. In addition, most primate social groups have been full of aggression from males and females alike (Sapolsky 2006). And in the hominid and then human hunter-gatherer bands of the past couple million years, violence has been a leading cause of death for men (Bowles 2006). We became anxious for good reason: there was a lot to fear.

SENSITIVITY TO NEGATIVE INFORMATION

The brain typically detects negative information faster than positive information. Take facial expressions, a primary signal of threat or opportunity for a social animal like us: fearful faces are perceived much more rapidly than happy or neutral ones, probably fast-tracked by the amygdala (Yang, Zald, and Blake 2007). In fact, even when researchers make fearful faces invisible to conscious awareness, the amygdala still lights up (Jiang and He 2006). The brain is *drawn* to bad news.

HIGH-PRIORITY STORAGE

When an event is flagged as negative, the hippocampus makes sure it's stored carefully for future reference. Once burned, twice shy. Your brain is like Velcro for negative experiences and Teflon for positive ones—even though most of your experiences are probably neutral or positive.

NEGATIVE TRUMPS POSITIVE

Negative events generally have more impact than positive ones. For example, it's easy to acquire feelings of learned helplessness from a few failures, but hard to undo those feelings, even with many successes (Seligman 2006). People will do more to avoid a loss than to acquire a comparable gain (Baumeister et al. 2001). Compared to lottery winners, accident victims usually take longer to return to their original baseline of happiness (Brickman, Coates, and Janoff-Bulman 1978). Bad information about a person carries more weight than good information (Peeters and Czapinski 1990), and in relationships, it typically takes about five positive interactions to overcome the effects of a single negative one (Gottman 1995).

LINGERING TRACES

Even if you've unlearned a negative experience, it still leaves an indelible trace in your brain (Quirk, Repa, and LeDoux 1995). That residue lies waiting, ready to reactivate if you ever encounter a fear-provoking event like the previous one.

VICIOUS CYCLES

Negative experiences create vicious cycles by making you pessimistic, overreactive, and inclined to go negative yourself.

Avoiding Involves Suffering

As you can see, your brain has a built-in "negativity bias" (Vaish, Grossman, and Woodward 2008) that primes you for avoidance. This bias makes you suffer in a variety of ways. For starters, it generates an unpleasant background of anxiety, which for some people can be quite intense; anxiety also makes it harder to bring attention inward for self-awareness or contemplative practice, since the brain keeps scanning to make sure there is no problem. The negativity bias fosters or intensifies other unpleasant emotions, such as anger, sorrow, depression, guilt, and shame. It highlights past losses and failures, it downplays present abilities, and it exaggerates future obstacles. Consequently, the mind continually tends to render unfair verdicts about a person's character, conduct, and possibilities. The weight of those judgments can really wear you down.

IN THE SIMULATOR

In Buddhism, it's said that suffering is the result of craving expressed through the Three Poisons: greed, hatred, and delusion. These are strong, traditional terms that cover a broad range of thoughts, words, and deeds, including the most fleeting and subtle. Greed is a grasping after carrots, while hatred is an aversion to sticks; both involve craving more pleasure and less pain. Delusion is a holding onto ignorance about the way things really are—for example, not seeing how they're connected and changing.

Virtual Reality

Sometimes these poisons are conspicuous; much of the time, however, they operate in the background of your awareness, firing and wiring quietly along. They do this by using your brain's extraordinary capacity to *represent* both inner experience and the outer world. For example, the blind spots in your left and right visual fields don't look like holes out there in the world; rather, your brain fills them in, much like photo software shades in the red eyes of people looking toward a flash. In fact, much of what you see "out there" is actually manufactured "in here" by your brain, painted in like computer-generated graphics in a movie. Only a small fraction of the inputs to your occipital lobe comes directly from the external world; the rest comes from internal memory stores and perceptual-processing modules (Raichle 2006). Your brain *simulates* the world—each of us lives in a virtual reality that's close enough to the real thing that we don't bump into the furniture.

Inside this simulator—whose neural substrate appears to be centered in the upper-middle of your PFC (Gusnard et al. 2001)—mini-movies run continuously. These brief clips are the building blocks of much conscious mental activity (Niedenthal 2007; Pitcher et al. 2008). For our ancestors, running simulations of past events promoted survival, as it strengthened the learning of successful behaviors by repeating their neural firing patterns. Simulating future events also promoted survival by enabling our ancestors to compare possible outcomes—in order to pick the best approach—and to ready potential sensory-motor sequences for immediate action. Over the past three million years, the brain has tripled in size; much of this expansion has improved the capabilities of the simulator, suggesting its benefits for survival.

Simulations Make You Suffer

The brain continues to produce simulations today, even when they have nothing to do with staying alive. Watch yourself daydream or go back over a relationship problem, and you'll see the clips playing—little packets of simulated experiences, usually just seconds long. If you observe them closely, you'll spot several troubling things:

- By its very nature, the simulator pulls you out of the present moment. There you are, following a presentation at work, running an errand, or meditating, and suddenly your mind is a thousand miles away, caught up in a mini-movie. But it's only in the present moment that we find real happiness, love, or wisdom.

- In the simulator, pleasures usually seem pretty great, whether you're considering a second cupcake or imagining the response you'll get to a report at work. But what do you *actually* feel when you enact the mini-movie in real life? Is it as pleasant as promised up there on the screen? Usually not. In truth, most everyday rewards aren't as intense as those conjured up in the simulator.

- Clips in the simulator contain lots of beliefs: *Of course he'll say X if I say Y....It's obvious that they let me down.* Sometimes these are explicitly verbalized, but much of the time they're implicit, built into the plotline. In reality, are the explicit and implicit beliefs in your simulations *true*? Sometimes yes, but often no. Mini-movies keep us stuck by their simplistic view of the past and by their defining out of existence real possibilities for the future, such as new ways to reach out to others or dream big dreams. Their beliefs are the bars of an invisible cage, trapping you in a life that's smaller than the one you could actually have. It's like being a zoo animal that's released into a large park—yet still crouches within the confines of its old pen.

- In the simulator, upsetting events from the past play again and again, which unfortunately strengthens the neural associations between an event and its painful feelings. The simulator also forecasts threatening situations in your future. But in fact, most of those worrisome events never materialize. And of the ones that do, often the discomfort you experience is milder and briefer than predicted. For example, imagine speaking from your heart: this may trigger a mini-movie ending in rejection and you feeling bad. But in fact, when you do speak from the heart, doesn't it typically go pretty well, with you ending up feeling quite good?

In sum, the simulator takes you out of the present moment and sets you chasing after carrots that aren't really so great while ignoring more important rewards (such as contentment and inner peace). Its mini-movies are full of limiting beliefs. Besides reinforcing painful emotions, they have you ducking sticks that never actually come your way or aren't really all that bad. And the simulator does this hour after hour, day after day, even in your dreams—steadily building neural structure, much of which adds to your suffering.

SELF-COMPASSION

Each person suffers sometimes, and many people suffer a lot. Compassion is a natural response to suffering, including your own. Self-compassion isn't self-pity, but is simply warmth, concern, and good wishes—just like compassion for another person. Because self-compassion is more emotional than self-esteem, it's actually more

> *The root of compassion is compassion for oneself.*
> —Pema Chödrön

powerful for reducing the impact of difficult conditions, preserving self-worth, and building resilience (Leary et al. 2007). It also opens your heart, since when you're closed to your own suffering, it's hard to be receptive to suffering in others.

In addition to the everyday suffering of life, the path of awakening itself contains difficult experiences which also call for compassion. To become happier, wiser, and more loving, sometimes you have to swim against ancient currents within your nervous system. For example, in some ways the three pillars of practice are unnatural: virtue restrains emotional reactions that worked well on the Serengeti, mindfulness decreases external vigilance, and wisdom cuts through beliefs that once helped us survive. It goes against the evolutionary template to undo the causes of suffering, to feel one with all things, to flow with the changing moment, and to remain unmoved by pleasant and unpleasant alike. Of course, that doesn't mean we shouldn't do it! It just means we should understand what we're up against and have some compassion for ourselves.

To nurture self-compassion and strengthen its neural circuits:

- Recall being with someone who really loves you—the feeling of receiving caring activates the deep attachment system circuitry in your brain, priming it to give compassion.

- Bring to mind someone you naturally feel compassion for, such as a child or a person you love—this easy flow of compassion arouses its neural underpinnings (including oxytocin, the *insula* [which senses the internal state of your body], and the PFC), "warming them up" for self-compassion.

- Extend this same compassion to yourself—be aware of your own suffering and extend concern and good wishes toward yourself; sense compassion sifting down into raw places inside, falling like a gentle rain that touches everything. The actions related to a feeling strengthen it (Niedenthal 2007), so place your palm on your cheek or heart with the tenderness and warmth you'd give a hurt child. Say phrases in your mind such as *May I be happy again. May the pain of this moment pass.*

• Overall, open to the sense that you are receiving compassion—deep down in your brain, the actual source of good feelings doesn't matter much; whether the compassion is from you or from another person, let your sense of being soothed and cared for sink in.

---

chapter 2: KEY POINTS

❀ Three fundamental strategies have evolved to help us pass on our genes: creating separations, stabilizing systems, and approaching opportunities while avoiding threats.

❀ Although these strategies are very effective for survival, they also make you suffer.

❀ The effort to maintain separations is at odds with the myriad ways you're actually connected with the world and dependent upon it. As a result, you may feel subtly isolated, alienated, overwhelmed, or as if you're in a struggle with the world.

❀ When the systems within your body, mind, and relationships become unstable, your brain produces uncomfortable signals of threat. Since everything keeps changing, these signals keep coming.

🪷 Your brain colors your experiences with a feeling tone—pleasant, unpleasant, or neutral—so you'll approach what's pleasant, avoid what's unpleasant, and move on from what's neutral.

🪷 In particular, we evolved to pay great attention to unpleasant experiences. This negativity bias overlooks good news, highlights bad news, and creates anxiety and pessimism.

🪷 The brain has a wonderful capacity to simulate experiences, but there's a price: the simulator pulls you out of the moment, plus it sets you chasing pleasures that aren't that great and resisting pains that are exaggerated or not even real.

🪷 Compassion for yourself helps reduce your suffering.

chapter 3

The First and Second Dart

*Ultimately, happiness comes down to choosing between
the discomfort of becoming aware of your mental afflictions
and the discomfort of being ruled by them.*

—Yongey Mingyur Rinpoche

Some physical discomfort is unavoidable; it's a crucial signal to take action to protect life and limb, like the pain that makes you pull your hand back from a hot stove. Some mental discomfort is inevitable, too. For example, as we evolved, growing emotional investments in children and other members of the band motivated our ancestors to keep those carriers of their genes alive; understandably, then, we feel distress when dear ones are threatened and sorrow when they are harmed. We also evolved to care greatly about our place in the band and in the hearts of others, so it's normal to feel hurt if you're rejected or scorned.

To borrow an expression from the Buddha, inescapable physical or mental discomfort is the "first dart" of existence. As long as you live and love, some of those darts will come your way.

THE DARTS WE THROW OURSELVES

First darts are unpleasant to be sure. But then we add our *reactions* to them. These reactions are "second darts"—the ones we throw ourselves. Most of our suffering comes from second darts.

Suppose you're walking through a dark room at night and stub your toe on a chair; right after the first dart of pain comes a second dart of anger: "Who moved that darn chair?!" Or maybe a loved one is cold to you when you're hoping for some caring; in addition to the natural drop in the pit of your stomach (first dart), you might feel unwanted (second dart) as a result of having been ignored as a child.

Second darts often trigger more second darts through associative neural networks: you might feel guilt about your anger that someone moved the chair, or sadness that you feel hurt yet again by someone you love. In relationships, second darts create vicious cycles: your second-dart reactions trigger reactions from the other person, which set off more second darts from you, and so on.

Remarkably, most of our second-dart reactions occur when there is in fact no first dart anywhere to be found—when there's no pain inherent in the conditions we're reacting to. We *add* suffering to them. For example, sometimes I'll come home from work and the house will be a mess, with the kids' stuff all over. That's the condition. Is there a first dart *in* the coats and shoes on the sofa or the clutter covering the counter? No, there isn't; no one dropped a brick on me or hurt my children. Do I *have* to get upset? Not really. I could ignore the stuff, pick it up calmly, or talk with them about it. Sometimes I manage to handle it that way. But if I don't, then the second darts start landing, tipped with the Three Poisons: greed makes me rigid about how I want things to be, hatred gets me all bothered and angry, and delusion tricks me into taking the situation personally.

Saddest of all, some second-dart reactions are to conditions that are actually *positive*. If someone pays you a compliment, that's a positive situation. But then you might start thinking, with some nervousness and even a little shame: *Oh, I'm not really that good a person. Maybe they'll find out I'm a fraud.* Right there, needless second-dart suffering begins.

HEATING UP

Suffering is not abstract or conceptual. It's *embodied:* you feel it in your body, and it proceeds through bodily mechanisms. Understanding the physical machinery of suffering will help you see it increasingly as an impersonal condition—unpleasant to be sure, but not worth getting upset about, which would just bring more second darts.

Suffering cascades through your body via the sympathetic nervous system (SNS) and the *hypothalamic-pituitary-adrenal axis* (HPAA) of the endocrine (hormonal) system. Let's unscramble this alphabet soup to see how it all works. While the SNS and HPAA are anatomically distinct, they are so intertwined that they're best described together, as an integrated system. And we'll focus on reactions dominated by an aversion to sticks (e.g., fear, anger) rather than a grasping for carrots, since aversive reactions usually have a bigger impact due to the negativity bias of the brain.

Alarms Go Off

Something happens. It might be a car suddenly cutting you off, a put-down from a coworker, or even just a worrisome thought. Social and emotional conditions can pack a wallop like physical ones since psychological pain draws on many of the same neural networks as physical pain (Eisenberger and Lieberman 2004); this is why getting rejected can feel as bad as a root canal. Even just anticipating a challenging event—such as giving a talk next week—can have as much impact as living through it for real. Whatever the source of the threat, the amygdala sounds the alarm, setting off several reactions:

- The *thalamus*—the relay station in the middle of your head—sends a "Wake up!" signal to your brain stem, which in turn releases stimulating norepinephrine throughout your brain.

- The SNS sends signals to the major organs and muscle groups in your body, readying them for fighting or fleeing.

- The hypothalamus—the brain's primary regulator of the endocrine system—prompts the pituitary gland to signal the adrenal glands to release the "stress hormones" *epinephrine (adrenaline)* and *cortisol.*

Ready for Action

Within a second or two of the initial alarm, your brain is on red alert, your SNS is lit up like a Christmas tree, and stress hormones are washing through your blood. In other words, you're at least a little upset. What's going on in your body?

Epinephrine increases your heart rate (so your heart can move more blood) and dilates your pupils (so your eyes gather more light). Norepinephrine shunts blood to large muscle groups. Meanwhile, the bronchioles of your lungs dilate for increased gas exchange—enabling you to hit harder or run faster.

Cortisol suppresses the immune system to reduce inflammation from wounds. It also revs up stress reactions in two circular ways: First, it causes the brain stem to stimulate the amygdala further, which increases amygdala activation of the SNS/HPAA system—which produces more cortisol. Second, cortisol suppresses hippocampal activity (which normally inhibits the amygdala); this takes the brakes off the amygdala, leading to yet more cortisol.

Reproduction is sidelined—no time for sex when you're running for cover. The same for digestion: salivation decreases and peristalsis slows down, so your mouth feels dry and you become constipated.

Your emotions intensify, organizing and mobilizing the whole brain for action. SNS/HPAA arousal stimulates the amygdala, which is hardwired to focus on negative information and react intensely to it. Consequently, feeling stressed sets you up for fear and anger.

As limbic and endocrine activation increases, the relative strength of executive control from the PFC declines. It's like being in a car with a runaway accelerator: the driver has less control over her vehicle. Further, the PFC is also affected by SNS/HPAA arousal, which pushes appraisals, attributions of others' intentions, and priorities in a negative direction: now the driver of the careening car thinks everybody else is an idiot. For example, consider the difference between your take on a situation when you're upset and your thoughts about it later when you're calmer.

In the harsh physical and social environments in which we evolved, this activation of multiple bodily systems helped our ancestors survive. But what's the cost of this today, with the chronic low-grade stresses of modern life?

Key Parts of Your Brain

Each of these parts of your brain does many things; the functions listed here are those relevant to this book.

- **Prefrontal cortex (PFC)**—sets goals, makes plans, directs action; shapes emotions, in part by guiding and sometimes inhibiting the limbic system

- **Anterior (frontal) cingulate cortex (ACC)**—steadies attention and monitors plans; helps integrate thinking and feeling (Yamasaki, LaBar, and McCarthy 2002); a "cingulate" is a curved bundle of nerve fibers

---

- **Insula**—senses the internal state of your body, including gut feelings; helps you be empathic; located on the inside of the temporal lobes on each side of your head (temporal lobes and insula not shown in figure 6)

- **Thalamus**—the major relay station for sensory information

- **Brain stem**—sends neuromodulators such as serotonin and dopamine to the rest of the brain

- **Corpus callosum**—passes information between the two hemispheres of the brain

- **Cerebellum**—regulates movement

- **Limbic system**—central to emotion and motivation; includes the basal ganglia, hippocampus, amygdala, hypothalamus, and pituitary gland; sometimes also considered to include parts of the cortex (e.g., cingulate, insula), but for simplicity we will

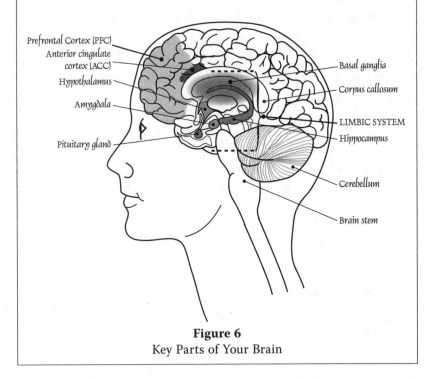

Figure 6
Key Parts of Your Brain

define it anatomically in terms of subcortical structures; many parts of the brain besides the limbic system are involved with emotion

- **Basal ganglia**—involved with rewards, stimulation seeking, and movement; "ganglia" are masses of tissue

- **Hippocampus**—forms new memories; detects threats

- **Amygdala**—a kind of "alarm bell" that responds particularly to emotionally charged or negative stimuli (Rasia-Filho, Londero, and Achaval 2000)

- **Hypothalamus**—regulates primal drives such as hunger and sex; makes oxytocin; activates the pituitary gland

- **Pituitary gland**—makes endorphins; triggers stress hormones; stores and releases oxytocin

LIFE ON SIMMER

Getting fired up for good reason—such as becoming passionate and enthusiastic, handling emergencies, or being forceful for a good cause—definitely has its place in life. But second darts are a bad reason to light up the SNS/HPAA system, and if they become routine, they can push the needle on your personal stress meter into the red zone. Further, apart from your individual situation, we live in a pedal-to-the-metal society that relies on nonstop SNS/HPAA activation; unfortunately, this is completely unnatural in terms of our evolutionary template.

For all of these reasons, most of us experience ongoing SNS/HPAA arousal. Even if your pot isn't boiling over, just simmering along with second-dart activation is quite unhealthy. It continually shunts resources away from long-term projects—such as building a strong immune system or preserving a good mood—in favor of short-term crises. And this has lasting consequences.

Physical Consequences

In our evolutionary past, when most people died by forty or so, the short-term benefits of SNS/HPAA activation outweighed its long-term costs. But for people today who are interested in living well during their forties and beyond, the accumulating damage of an overheated life is a real concern. For example, chronic SNS/HPAA stimulation disturbs these systems and increases risks for the health problems listed (Licinio, Gold, and Wong 1995; Sapolsky 1998; Wolf 1995):

- **Gastrointestinal**—ulcers, colitis, irritable bowel syndrome, diarrhea, and constipation

- **Immune**—more frequent colds and flus, slower wound healing, greater vulnerability to serious infections

- **Cardiovascular**—hardening of the arteries, heart attacks

- **Endocrine**—type II diabetes, premenstrual syndrome, erectile dysfunction, lowered libido

Mental Consequences

For all their effects on the body, second darts usually have their greatest impact on psychological well-being. Let's see how they work in your brain to raise anxiety and lower mood.

ANXIETY

Repeated SNS/HPAA activity makes the amygdala more reactive to apparent threats, which in turn increases SNS/HPAA activation, which sensitizes the amygdala further. The mental correlate of this physical process is an increasingly rapid arousal of *state anxiety* (anxiety based on specific situations). Additionally, the amygdala helps form *implicit memories* (traces of past experiences that exist beneath conscious awareness); as it becomes more sensitized, it increasingly shades those residues with fear, thus intensifying *trait anxiety* (ongoing anxiety regardless of the situation).

Meanwhile, frequent SNS/HPAA activation wears down the hippocampus, which is vital for forming *explicit memories*—clear records of what actually happened. Cortisol and related glucocorticoid hormones both weaken existing synaptic connections in the hippocampus and inhibit the formation of new ones. Further, the hippocampus is one of the few regions in the human brain that can actually grow new neurons—yet glucocorticoids prevent the birth of neurons in the hippocampus, impairing its ability to produce new memories.

It's a bad combination for the amygdala to be oversensitized while the hippocampus is compromised: painful experiences can then be recorded in implicit memory—with all the distortions and turbo-charging of an amygdala on overdrive—without an accurate explicit memory of them. This might feel like: *Something happened, I'm not sure what, but I'm really upset.* This may help explain why victims of trauma can feel dissociated from the awful things they experienced, yet be very reactive to any trigger that reminds them unconsciously of what once occurred. In less extreme situations, the one-two punch of a revved-up amygdala and a weakened hippocampus can lead to feeling a little upset a lot of the time without exactly knowing why.

DEPRESSED MOOD

Routine SNS/HPAA activation undermines the biochemical basis of an even-keeled—let alone cheerful—disposition in a number of ways:

- Norepinephrine helps you feel alert and mentally energetic, but glucocorticoid hormones deplete it. Reduced norepinephrine may cause you to feel flat—even apathetic—with poor concentration; these are classic symptoms of depression.

- Over time, glucocorticoids lower the production of dopamine. This leads to a loss of enjoyment of activities once found pleasurable: another classic criterion for depression.

- Stress reduces serotonin, probably the most important neurotransmitter for maintaining a good mood. When serotonin drops, so does norepinephrine, which has already been diminished by glucocorticoids. In short, less serotonin means more vulnerability to a blue mood and less alert interest in the world.

An Intimate Process

Of course, our experience of these physiological processes is very intimate. When I'm upset, I sure don't think about all of these biochemical details. But having a general idea of them in the back of my mind helps me appreciate the sheer physicality of a second dart cascade, its impersonal nature and dependence on preceding causes, and its impermanence.

This understanding is hopeful and motivating. Suffering has clear causes in your brain and body, so if you change its causes, you'll suffer a lot less. And you *can* change those causes. From this point on, we're going to focus on how to do just that.

THE PARASYMPATHETIC NERVOUS SYSTEM

So far, we've examined how reactions powered by greed and hatred—especially the latter—ripple through your brain and body, shaped by the sympathetic nervous system. But the SNS is just one of the three wings of the *autonomic nervous system* (ANS), which operates mostly below the level of consciousness to regulate many bodily systems and their responses to changing conditions. The other two wings of the ANS are the *parasympathetic nervous system* (PNS) and the *enteric nervous system* (which regulates your gastrointestinal system). Let's focus on the PNS and SNS as they play crucial roles in your suffering—and its end.

The PNS conserves energy in your body and is responsible for ongoing, steady-state activity. It produces a feeling of relaxation, often with a sense of contentment—this is why it's sometimes called the "rest-and-digest" system, in contrast to the "fight-or-flight" SNS. These two wings of the ANS are connected like a seesaw: when one goes up, the other one goes down.

Parasympathetic activation is the normal resting state of your body, brain, and mind. If your SNS were surgically disconnected, you'd stay alive (though you wouldn't be very useful in an emergency). If your PNS were disconnected, however, you'd stop breathing and soon die. Sympathetic activation is a *change* to the baseline of PNS equilibrium in order to respond to a threat or an opportunity. The cooling, steadying influence of the PNS helps you think clearly and avoid hot-headed actions that would harm you or others. The PNS also quiets the mind and fosters tranquility, which supports contemplative insight.

THE BIG PICTURE

The PNS and SNS evolved hand in hand in order to keep animals— including humans—alive in potentially lethal environments. We need both of them.

For example, take five breaths, inhaling and exhaling a little more fully than usual. This is both energizing and relaxing, activating first the sympathetic system and then the parasympathetic one, back and forth, in a gentle rhythm. Notice how you feel when you're done. That combination of aliveness and centeredness is the essence of the peak performance zone recognized by athletes, businesspeople, artists, lovers, and meditators. It's the result of the SNS and PNS, the gas pedal and the brakes, working in harmony together.

Happiness, love, and wisdom aren't furthered by shutting down the SNS, but rather by keeping the autonomic nervous system as a whole in an optimal state of balance:

- Mainly parasympathetic arousal for a baseline of ease and peacefulness

- Mild SNS activation for enthusiasm, vitality, and wholesome passions

- Occasional SNS spikes to deal with demanding situations, from a great opportunity at work to a late-night call from a teenager who needs a ride home from a party gone bad

This is your best-odds prescription for a long, productive, happy life. Of course, it takes practice.

A PATH OF PRACTICE

As the saying goes, pain is inevitable but suffering is optional. If you can simply stay present with whatever is arising in awareness—whether it's a first dart or a second one—without reacting further, then you will break the chain of suffering right there. Over time, through training and shaping your mind and brain, you can even change what arises, increasing what's positive and decreasing what's negative. In the meantime, you can rest in and be nourished by a growing sense of the peace and clarity in your true nature.

These three processes—*being with* whatever arises, *working with* the tendencies of mind to transform them, and *taking refuge* in the ground of being—are the essential practices of the path of awakening. In many ways they correspond, respectively, to mindfulness, virtue, and wisdom—and to the three fundamental neural functions of learning, regulating, and selecting.

As you deal with different issues on your path of awakening, you'll repeatedly encounter these stages of growth:

- *Stage one*—you're caught in a second-dart reaction and don't even realize it: your partner forgets to bring milk home and you complain angrily without seeing that your reaction is over the top.

- *Stage two*—you realize you've been hijacked by greed or hatred (in the broadest sense), but cannot help yourself: internally you're squirming, but you can't stop grumbling bitterly about the milk.

- *Stage three*—some aspect of the reaction arises, but you don't act it out: you feel irritated but remind yourself that your partner does a lot for you already and getting cranky will just make things worse.

- *Stage four*—the reaction doesn't even come up, and sometimes you forget you ever had the issue: you understand that there's no milk, and you calmly figure out what to do now with your partner.

In education, these are known succinctly as unconscious incompetence, conscious incompetence, conscious competence, and unconscious competence. They're useful labels for knowing where you are with a given issue. The second stage is the hardest one, and often where we want to quit. So it's important to keep aiming for the third and fourth stages—just keep at it and you'll definitely get there!

It takes effort and time to clear old structures and build new ones. I call this *the law of little things*: although little moments of greed, hatred, and delusion have left residues of suffering in your mind and brain, lots of little moments of practice will replace these

Three Poisons and the suffering they cause with happiness, love, and wisdom.

We've covered a lot of ground and have seen a lot about the evolutionary origins and neural causes of suffering. Now, in the rest of this book, let's see how to end it.

chapter 3: KEY POINTS

🪷 Some physical and mental discomforts are unavoidable. These are the "first darts" of life.

🪷 When we react to a first dart with one or more of the Three Poisons of greed, hatred, and delusion (broadly defined)—each one of which has craving at its center—we start throwing second darts at ourselves and others. In fact, we often toss second darts even when no first dart is to be found. Most poignantly, we sometimes throw second darts as a reaction to situations that are actually good, such as receiving a compliment.

🪷 Suffering is deeply embodied. Physical reactions involving your sympathetic nervous system (SNS) and hypothalamic-pituitary-adrenal axis (HPAA) cause suffering to snowball throughout your body.

🪷 Most people experience chronic second-dart cascades, with numerous negative consequences for their physical and mental health.

🪷 The rest-and-digest parasympathetic nervous system (PNS) calms down SNS/HPAA activation.

🪷 The best-odds prescription for a long, good life is a baseline of mainly PNS arousal with mild SNS activation for vitality, combined with occasional SNS spikes for major opportunities or threats.

❀ Being with whatever arises, working with the tendencies of mind to transform them, and taking refuge in the ground of being are the essential practices of the path of awakening. In many ways, these practices correspond, respectively, to mindfulness, virtue, and wisdom.

❀ On the path of awakening, keep going! Lots of little moments of practice will gradually and truly increase your contentment, kindness, and insight.

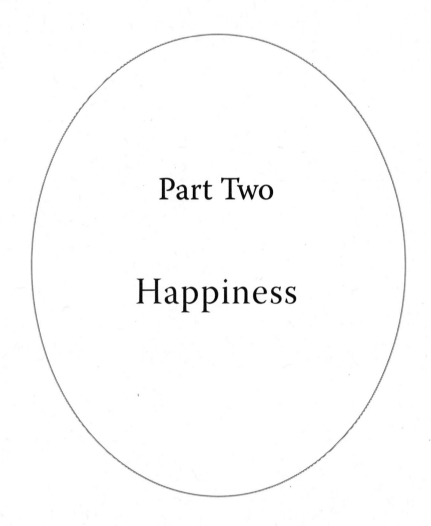

Part Two

Happiness

chapter 4

Taking in the Good

I am larger, better than I thought,
I did not know I held so much goodness.

—Walt Whitman, "Song of the Open Road"

Much as your body is built from the foods you eat, your mind is built from the experiences you have. The flow of experience gradually sculpts your brain, thus shaping your mind. Some of the results can be explicitly recalled: *This is what I did last summer; that is how I felt when I was in love.* But most of the shaping of your mind remains forever unconscious. This is called implicit memory, and it includes your expectations, models of relationships, emotional tendencies, and general outlook. Implicit memory establishes the interior landscape of your mind—what it feels like to be you—based on the slowly accumulating residues of lived experience.

In a sense, those residues can be sorted into two piles: those that benefit you and others, and those that cause harm. To paraphrase the Wise Effort section of Buddhism's Noble Eightfold Path, you should create, preserve, and increase beneficial implicit memories, and prevent, eliminate, or decrease harmful ones.

THE NEGATIVITY BIAS OF MEMORY

But here's the problem: your brain preferentially scans for, registers, stores, recalls, and reacts to unpleasant experiences; as we've said, it's like Velcro for negative experiences and Teflon for positive ones. Consequently, even when positive experiences outnumber negative ones, the pile of negative implicit memories naturally grows faster. Then the background feeling of what it feels like to be you can become undeservedly glum and pessimistic.

Sure, negative experiences do have benefits: loss opens the heart, remorse provides a moral compass, anxiety alerts you to threats, and anger spotlights wrongs that should be righted. But do you really think you're not having enough negative experiences?! Emotional pain with no benefit to yourself or others is pointless suffering. And pain today breeds more pain tomorrow. For instance, even a single episode of major depression can reshape circuits of the brain to make future episodes more likely (Maletic et al. 2007).

The remedy is not to suppress negative experiences; when they happen, they happen. Rather, it is to foster positive experiences—and in particular, to take them in so they become a permanent part of you.

INTERNALIZING THE POSITIVE

Here's how, in three steps:

1. Turn positive facts into positive *experiences*. Good things keep happening all around us, but much of the time we don't notice them; even when we do, we often hardly feel them. Someone is nice to you, you see an admirable quality in yourself, a flower is blooming, you finish a difficult project—and it all just rolls by. Instead, actively look for good news, particularly the little stuff of daily life: the faces of children, the smell of an orange, a memory from a happy vacation, a minor success at

work, and so on. Whatever positive facts you find, bring a mindful awareness to them—open up to them and let them affect you. It's like sitting down to a banquet: don't just look at it—dig in!

2. Savor the experience. It's delicious! Make it last by staying with it for 5, 10, even 20 seconds; don't let your attention skitter off to something else. The longer that something is held in awareness and the more emotionally stimulating it is, the more neurons that fire and thus wire together, and the stronger the trace in memory (Lewis 2005).

   Focus on your emotions and body sensations, since these are the essence of implicit memory. Let the experience fill your body and be as intense as possible. For example, if someone is good to you, let the feeling of being cared about bring warmth to your whole chest.

   Pay particular attention to the rewarding aspects of the experience—for example, how good it feels to get a great big hug from someone you love. Focusing on these rewards increases dopamine release, which makes it easier to keep giving the experience your attention, and strengthens its neural associations in implicit memory. You're not doing this to cling to the rewards—which would eventually make you suffer—but rather to internalize them so that you carry them inside you and don't need to reach for them in the outer world.

   You can also intensify an experience by deliberately enriching it. For example, if you are savoring a relationship experience, you could call up other feelings of being loved by others, which will help stimulate oxytocin— the "bonding hormone"—and thus deepen your sense of connection. Or you could strengthen your feelings of satisfaction after completing a demanding project by thinking about some of the challenges you had to overcome.

3. Imagine or feel that the experience is entering deeply into your mind and body, like the sun's warmth into a T-shirt, water into a sponge, or a jewel placed in a treasure chest in your heart. Keep relaxing your body and absorbing the emotions, sensations, and thoughts of the experience.

HEALING PAIN

Positive experiences can also be used to soothe, balance, and even replace negative ones. When two things are held in mind at the same time, they start to connect with each other. That's one reason why talking about hard things with someone who's supportive can be so healing: painful feelings and memories get infused with the comfort, encouragement, and closeness you experience with the other person.

Using the Machinery of Memory

These mental minglings draw on the neural machinery of memory. When a memory—whether implicit or explicit—is made, only its key features are stored, not every single detail. Otherwise, your brain would become so crowded that it wouldn't have space to learn anything new. For example, remember an experience, even a recent one, and notice how schematic your recollection is, with the main features sketched in but many details left out.

When your brain retrieves a memory, it does not do it like a computer does, which calls up a complete record of what's on its hard drive (e.g., document, picture, song). Your brain rebuilds implicit and explicit memories from their key features, drawing on its simulating capacities to fill in missing details. While this is more work, it's also a more efficient use of neural real estate—this way complete records don't need to be stored. And your brain is so fast that you don't notice the regeneration of each memory.

This rebuilding process gives you the opportunity, right down in the micro-circuitry of your brain, to gradually shift the emotional shadings of your interior landscape. When a memory is activated, a large-scale assembly of neurons and synapses forms an emergent pattern. If other things are in your mind at the same time—and particularly if they're strongly pleasant or unpleasant—your amygdala and hippocampus will automatically associate them with that neural pattern (Pare, Collins, and Pelletier 2002). Then, when the memory leaves awareness, it will be reconsolidated in storage *along with those other associations.*

The next time the memory is activated, it will tend to bring those associations with it. Thus, if you repeatedly bring to mind negative feelings and thoughts while a memory is active, then that memory will be increasingly shaded in a negative direction. For example, recalling an old failure while simultaneously lambasting yourself will make that failure seem increasingly awful. On the other hand, if you call up positive emotions and perspectives while implicit or explicit memories are active, these wholesome influences will slowly be woven into the fabric of those memories.

Every time you do this—every time you sift positive feelings and views into painful, limiting states of mind—you build a little bit of neural structure. Over time, the accumulating impact of this positive material will literally, synapse by synapse, change your brain.

Lifelong Learning

- Neural circuits started forming before you were born, and your brain will keep learning and changing up to your very last breath.

- Humans have the longest childhood of any animal on the planet. Since children are very vulnerable in the wild, there must have been a large evolutionary payoff in giving the brain an extended period of intense development. Of course, learning continues after childhood; we continually acquire new skills and knowledge all the way into old age. (After he turned 90,

---

my dad made my jaw drop with an article in which he calcu-
lated the best odds for different bids in bridge; there are lots of
similar examples.)

- The brain's capacity to learn—and thus change itself—is called
  neuroplasticity. Usually, the results are tiny, incremental alter-
  nations in neural structure that add up as the years go by.
  Occasionally, the results are dramatic—for example, in blind
  people, some occipital regions designed for visual processing
  can be rezoned for auditory functions (Begley 2007).

- Mental activity shapes neural structure in a variety of ways:

  - Neurons that are particularly active become even more
    responsive to input.

  - Busy neural networks receive increased blood flow,
    which supplies them with more glucose and oxygen.

  - When neurons fire together—within a few milliseconds
    of each other—they strengthen their existing synapses
    and form new ones; this is how they "wire" together
    (Tanaka et al. 2008).

  - Inactive synapses wither away through *neuronal
    pruning*, a kind of survival of the busiest: use it or lose it.
    A toddler has about three times as many synapses as an
    adult; on the way to adulthood, adolescents can lose up
    to 10,000 synapses per second in the prefrontal cortex
    (PFC) (Spear 2000).

  - Brand new neurons grow in the hippocampus; this *neu-
    rogenesis* increases the openness of memory networks to
    new learning (Gould et al. 1999).

- Emotional arousal facilitates learning by increasing neural
  excitation and consolidating synaptic change (Lewis 2005).

Because of all the ways your brain changes its structure, your
experience *matters* beyond its momentary, subjective impact. It

makes enduring changes in the physical tissues of your brain which affect your well-being, functioning, and relationships. Based on science, this is a fundamental reason for being kind to yourself, cultivating wholesome experiences, and taking them in.

Pulling Weeds and Planting Flowers

To gradually replace negative implicit memories with positive ones, just make the positive aspects of your experience prominent and relatively intense in the foreground of your awareness while simultaneously placing the negative material in the background. Imagine that the positive contents of your awareness are sinking down into old wounds, soothing chafed and bruised places like a warm golden salve, filling up hollows, slowly replacing negative feelings and beliefs with positive ones.

The negative mental material you're working with could be from adulthood, including current experiences. But it's often important to address explicit and implicit memories from your childhood, since these are usually the taproots of the things that keep upsetting you. People sometimes get angry with themselves about still being affected by things from the past. But remember: the brain is designed to change through experiences, especially negative ones; we learn from our experiences, particularly those that happened during childhood, and it is natural for that learning to stick with us.

Growing up, I used to weed dandelions in our front yard, and they'd always grow back if I didn't pull out their entire root. Upsets are like that, too. So sense down into the youngest, most vulnerable, most emotionally charged layers of your mind, and feel around for the tip of the root of whatever is bothering you. With a little practice and self-understanding, you'll develop a short list of "usual suspects"—the deep sources of your recurring upsets—and you'll start routinely considering them if you feel irritated, anxious, hurt, or inadequate. These deep sources might include feeling unwanted by others due to being unpopular in school, a sense of helplessness from a chronic illness, or mistrust of intimacy following a bad divorce. When you find the tip of the root, take in the good that will gradually dislodge its hold upon you. You'll be pulling weeds and planting flowers in the garden of your mind.

Painful experiences are often best healed by positive ones that are their opposite—for example, replacing childhood feelings of being weak with a current sense of strength. If sadness from mistreatment in an old relationship keeps coming up, recall being loved by other people, and let those feelings sink in. Add the power of language by saying something like this to yourself: *I got through all that, I'm still here, and many people love me.* You won't forget what happened, but its emotional charge will steadily diminish.

The point is not to resist painful experiences or grasp at pleasant ones: that's a kind of craving—and craving leads to suffering. The art is to find a balance in which you remain mindful, accepting, and curious regarding difficult experiences—while also taking in supportive feelings and thoughts.

In sum, infuse positive material into negative material in these two ways:

- When you have a positive experience today, help it sink in to old pains.

- When negative material arises, bring to mind the positive emotions and perspectives that will be its antidote.

Whenever you use one of these methods, try to feel and take in related positive experiences at least a couple more times within the following hour. There's evidence that negative memory—both explicit and implicit—is especially vulnerable to change soon after it's been recalled (Monfils et al. 2009).

If you're feeling ambitious, do something additional: take small risks and do things that reason tells you are fine but worry wants you to avoid—such as being more open about your true feelings, asking directly for love, or reaching higher in your career. When the results turn out to be good—as they most likely will—take them in and slowly but surely clear out those old fears.

Most of the time, taking in the good takes less than a minute— often, just a few seconds. It's a private act. No one needs to know you're doing it. But over time, you really can build new, positive structures in your brain.

WHY IT'S GOOD TO TAKE IN THE GOOD

Given the negativity bias of the brain, it takes an *active* effort to internalize positive experiences and heal negative ones. When you tilt toward what's positive, you're actually righting a neurological imbalance. And you're giving yourself today the caring and encouragement you should have received as a child, but perhaps didn't get in full measure.

Focusing on what is wholesome and then taking it in naturally increases the positive emotions flowing through your mind each day. Emotions have global effects since they organize the brain as a whole. Consequently, positive feelings have far-reaching benefits, including a stronger immune system (Frederickson 2000) and a cardiovascular system that is less reactive to stress (Frederickson and Levenson 1998). They lift your mood; increase optimism, resilience, and resourcefulness; and help counteract the effects of painful experiences, including trauma (Frederickson 2001; Frederickson et al. 2000). It's a positive cycle: good feelings today increase the likelihood of good feelings tomorrow.

These benefits apply to children as well. In particular, taking in the good has a special payoff for kids at either the spirited or the anxious end of the temperament spectrum. Spirited children usually zip along to the next thing before good feelings have a chance to consolidate in the brain, and anxious children tend to ignore or downplay good news. (And some kids are both spirited and anxious.) Whatever their temperament, if children are part of your life, encourage them to pause for a moment at the end of the day (or at any other natural interval, such as the last minute before the school bell) to remember what went well and think about things that make them happy (e.g., a pet, their parents' love, a goal scored in soccer). Then have those positive feelings and thoughts sink in.

In terms of spiritual practice, taking in the good highlights key states of mind, such as kindness and inner peace, so you can find your way back to them again. It is rewarding, and this helps keep you on the path of awakening, which does sometimes feel like an uphill slog. It builds conviction and faith by showing you the results of your efforts. It nourishes wholeheartedness through its emphasis on positive, heartfelt emotions—and when your own heart is full, you have more to offer to others.

Taking in the good is not about putting a happy shiny face on everything, nor is it about turning away from the hard things in life. It's about nourishing well-being, contentment, and peace inside that are refuges you can always come from and return to.

---

chapter 4: KEY POINTS

✿ Explicit memories are conscious recollections of specific events or other information. Implicit memories are residues of past experiences that largely remain below awareness but powerfully shape the inner landscape and atmosphere of your mind.

✿ Unfortunately, the bias of the brain tilts implicit memories in a negative direction, even when most of your experiences are actually positive.

✿ The first remedy is to consciously look for and take in positive experiences. There are three simple steps: turn positive facts into positive experiences, savor these experiences, and sense them sinking in.

✿ When experiences are consolidated in memory, they take with them whatever else is also in awareness, especially if it is intense. You can use this mechanism to infuse positive material into negative material; this is the second remedy. Simply have a positive experience be prominent in awareness while the painful one is sensed dimly in the background. Use this method in two ways: when you have a positive experience, help it sink into, soothe, and replace old pains; when negative material arises, bring to mind emotions and perspectives that are its antidote.

🪷 Become aware of the deep roots of recurring upsets; the tips of these roots are typically lodged in childhood experiences; different upsets may have different roots. Deliberately direct positive experiences toward these roots in order to pull them out completely and stop them from growing back.

🪷 Every time you take in the good, you build a little bit of neural structure. Doing this a few times a day—for months and even years—will gradually change your brain, and how you feel and act, in far-reaching ways.

🪷 It's good to take in the good. It builds up positive emotions, with many benefits for your physical and mental health. It's a great resource for children, especially spirited or anxious ones. And it aids spiritual practice by supporting motivation, conviction, and wholeheartedness.

chapter 5

Cooling the Fires

Indeed, the sage who's fully quenched
Rests at ease in every way;
No sense desire adheres to him
Whose fires have cooled, deprived of fuel.

All attachments have been severed,
The heart's been led away from pain;
Tranquil, he rests with utmost ease.
The mind has found its way to peace.

The Buddha (Cullavagga 6:4.4)

As we've seen, your sympathetic nervous system (SNS) and stress-related hormones "fire up" to help you pursue opportunities and avoid threats. While there's certainly a place for healthy passion and for strong stands against things that are harmful, most of the time we're just overheated—caught up with some carrot or struggling with some stick. Then we feel driven, rattled, stressed, irritated, anxious, or blue. Definitely not happy. We need to lower the flames. This chapter will cover many ways to do just that.

· If your body had a fire department, it would be the parasympathetic nervous system (PNS), so that's where we'll start.

ACTIVATING THE PARASYMPATHETIC NERVOUS SYSTEM

Your body has numerous major systems, including the endocrine (hormone), cardiovascular, immune, gastrointestinal, and nervous systems. If you want to use the mind-body connection to lower your stress, cool the fires, and improve your long-term health, what's the optimal point of entry into all of these systems? It's the autonomic nervous system (ANS).

This is because the ANS—which is part of the larger nervous system—is intertwined with and helps regulate every other system. And mental activity has greater direct influence over the ANS than any other bodily system. When you stimulate the parasympathetic wing of the ANS, calming, soothing, healing ripples spread through your body, brain, and mind.

Let's explore a variety of ways to light up the PNS.

Relaxation

Relaxing engages the circuitry of the PNS and thus strengthens it. Relaxing also quiets the fight-or-flight sympathetic nervous system, since relaxed muscles send feedback to the alarm centers in the brain that all is well. When you're very relaxed, it's hard to feel stressed or upset (Benson 2000). In fact, the relaxation response may actually alter how your genes are expressed, and thus reduce the cellular damage of chronic stress (Dusek et al. 2008).

You can reap the benefits of relaxation not only by initiating it in specific, stressful situations, but also by training your body "offline" to relax automatically; the methods that follow can be used in either way. First, here are four quick ones:

- Relax your tongue, eyes, and jaw muscles.

- Feel tension draining out of your body and sinking down into the earth.

- Run warm water over your hands.

- Scan your body for areas that are tense, and relax them.

DIAPHRAGM BREATHING

The next method—diaphragm breathing—takes a minute or two. The diaphragm is the muscle beneath your lungs that helps you breathe; actively working it is particularly effective for reducing anxiety.

Place your hand on your stomach a couple of inches beneath the upside-down V at the center of your rib cage. Look down, breathe normally, and watch your hand. You'll probably see it move only a little bit, and sort of up and down.

Leaving your hand in place, now breathe in such a way that your hand moves out and back, perpendicular to your chest. Try to breathe into your hand with real oomph, so that it travels back and forth half an inch or more with each breath.

This can take some practice, but keep at it and you'll get it. Next, try diaphragm breathing without your hand so you can use this method, if you like, in public settings.

PROGRESSIVE RELAXATION

If you have three to ten minutes, try progressive relaxation, in which you focus systematically on different parts of your body, working either from the feet to the head or vice versa. Depending on how much time you have, you might focus on large sections of your body—e.g., left leg, right leg—or on much smaller units, such as left foot, right foot, left ankle, right ankle, and so on. You can do progressive relaxation with your eyes open or closed, but learning to do it with your eyes open will help you relax more deeply if you're with other people.

In order to relax a part of your body, simply bring it into awareness; for example, take a moment right now to notice the sensations in the bottom of your left foot. Or say "relax" softly in your mind as you bring awareness to a body part. Or locate a point or a space in that part. Whatever works best.

For many people, progressive relaxation is also a great method for falling asleep.

Big Exhalation

Inhale as much as you can, hold that inhalation for a few seconds, and then exhale slowly while relaxing. A big inhalation really expands your lungs, requiring a big exhalation to bring the lungs back to their resting size. This stimulates the PNS, which is in charge of exhaling.

Touching the Lips

Parasympathetic fibers are spread throughout your lips; thus, touching your lips stimulates the PNS. Touching your lips can also bring up soothing associations of eating or even of breastfeeding when you were a baby.

Mindfulness of the Body

Since your PNS is primarily directed at maintaining the internal equilibrium of your body, bringing attention inward activates parasympathetic networks (as long as you're not worried about your health). You may have already had some practice with mindfulness of the body (e.g., yoga, a stress-management class). Mindfulness just means being fully aware of something, in the moment with it, and not judging or resisting it. Be attentive to physical sensations; that's all there is to it.

For example, notice the sensations of breathing, the cool air coming in and the warm air going out, the chest and belly rising and falling. Or the sensations of walking, reaching, or swallowing. Following even a single breath from beginning to end—or a single step on the way to work—can be remarkably centering and calming.

Imagery

Although mental activity is commonly equated with verbal thought, most of the brain is actually devoted to nonverbal activities, such as processing mental pictures. Imagery activates the right hemisphere of the brain and quiets internal verbal chatter that could be stressful.

Like relaxation, you can use imagery on the spot to stimulate the PNS, or do longer visualizations when you've got the time to develop imagery that will be a powerful anchor for well-being. For example, if you're feeling stressed while at work, you could bring to mind a peaceful mountain lake for a few seconds. Then, when you have more time at home, you might visualize walking around the lake, and enrich your mental movie with the good smells of pine needles or the sound of children laughing.

Balance Your Heartbeat

A regular heart rate has small changes in the interval between each beat; this is called *heart rate variability* (HRV). For example, if your heart beat sixty times in a minute, the time between beats would average one second. But your heart is not a mechanical metronome, and the interval between beats is continually changing: it could be something like 1 sec., 1.05 sec., 1.1 sec., 1.15 sec., 1.1 sec., 1.05 sec., 1 sec., .95 sec., .9 sec., .85 sec., .9 sec., .95 sec., 1 sec., and so on.

HRV reflects the activity of the autonomic nervous system. For example, your heart speeds up a little when you inhale (SNS activation) and slows down when you exhale (PNS arousal). Stress, negative emotions, and aging all decrease HRV, and people with relatively low HRV are less likely to recover after a heart attack (Kristal-Boneh, et al. 1995).

An interesting question is whether heart rate variability is merely an *effect* of ups and downs in stress and other factors, or whether changes in HRV can themselves directly *cause* improvements in mental and physical health. The evidence is preliminary, but studies have shown that learning to increase the amount and coherence of HRV is associated with decreased stress, and improved cardiovascular health, immune system function, and mood (Luskin, et al. 2002; McCraty, Atkinson, and Thomasino 2003).

HRV is a good indicator of parasympathetic arousal and overall well-being, and you can change it directly. The HeartMath Institute has pioneered the study of HRV and developed numerous techniques, which we've adapted for this simple, three-part approach:

1. Breathe in such a way that your inhalation and exhalation are the same duration; for example, count one, two, three, four in your mind while inhaling, and one, two, three, four while exhaling.

2. At the same time, imagine or sense that you're breathing in and out through the area of your heart.

3. As you breathe evenly through your heart, call to mind a pleasant, heartfelt emotion such as gratitude, kindness, or love—perhaps by thinking about a happy time, being with your children, appreciation for the good things in your life, or a pet. You can also imagine this feeling moving through your heart as part of the breath.

Try this for a minute or longer—you'll probably be quite struck by the results.

Meditation

Meditation activates the PNS through multiple pathways. These include withdrawing attention from stressful matters, relaxing, and bringing awareness into the body. Through stimulating the PNS and other parts of the nervous system, regular meditation:

- Increases gray matter in the insula (Hölzel et al. 2008; Lazar et al. 2005), hippocampus (Hölzel et al. 2008; Luders et al. 2009), and prefrontal cortex (Lazar et al. 2005; Luders et al. 2009); reduces cortical thinning due to aging in prefrontal regions strengthened by meditation (Lazar et al. 2008); improves psychological functions associated with these regions, including attention (Carter et al. 2005; Tang et al. 2007), compassion (Lutz, Brefczynski-Lewis et al. 2008), and empathy (Lazar et al. 2005)

- Increases activation of left frontal regions, which lifts mood (Davidson 2004)

- Increases the power and reach of fast, gamma-range brainwaves in experienced Tibetan practitioners (Lutz et al. 2004); brainwaves are the weak but measurable electrical waves produced by large numbers of neurons firing rhythmically together

- Decreases stress-related cortisol (Tang et al. 2007)

- Strengthens the immune system (Davidson et al. 2003; Tang et al. 2007)

- Helps a variety of medical conditions, including cardiovascular disease, asthma, type II diabetes, PMS, and chronic pain (Walsh and Shapiro 2006)

- Helps numerous psychological conditions, including insomnia, anxiety, phobias, and eating disorders (Walsh and Shapiro 2006)

There are many contemplative traditions and many ways to meditate, and you may already have your own favorite method. The following box describes a basic mindfulness meditation. The key to reaping the rewards of meditation is to develop a regular, daily practice, no matter how brief. How about making a personal commitment never to go to sleep without having meditated that day, even if for just one minute? Also consider joining a regular meditation group in your area.

Mindfulness Meditation

Find a comfortable place where you can focus and you won't be disturbed. It's fine to meditate while standing, walking, or lying down, but most people do so while sitting on a chair or cushion. Find a posture that is both relaxed and alert, with your spine reasonably straight. As the Zen saying suggests, you should handle your mind like the skillful rider of a horse, with neither too tight nor too loose a rein.

Meditate for as long as you like. You can start with shorter periods, even just five minutes. Longer sittings, from thirty to sixty minutes, will usually help you go deeper. You can decide how long you're going to meditate at the outset or play it by ear. It's all right to glance at a clock during the meditation. Alternately, you could set a timer. Some people light a stick of incense—when it's finished, they are, too. Feel free to modify the suggestions that follow.

Take a big breath and relax, with your eyes open or closed. Be aware of sounds coming and going, and let them be whatever they are. Know that you are taking this time to meditate. You can drop all other concerns during this period, like setting down

---

a heavy bag before plopping into a comfortable chair. After the meditation, you can pick those concerns up again—if you want to!

Bring your awareness to the sensations of breathing. Don't try to control the breath; let it be whatever it is. Sense the cool air coming in and warm air going out. The chest and belly rising and falling.

Try to stay with the sensations of each breath from beginning to end. You may want to softly count your breaths—count to ten and then start over; go back to one if your mind wanders—or note them quietly to yourself as "in" and "out." It's normal for the mind to wander, and when it does, just return to the breath. Be gentle and kind with yourself. See if you can stay attentive to ten breaths in a row (usually a challenge at first). After your mind settles down during the first minutes of the meditation, explore becoming increasingly absorbed in the breath and letting go of everything else. Open to the simple pleasures of breathing, given over to the breath. With some practice, see if you can stay present with the breath for dozens of breaths in a row.

Using the breath as a kind of anchor, be aware of whatever else is moving through the mind. Aware of thoughts and feelings, wishes and plans, images and memories—all coming and going. Let them be what they are; don't get caught up in them; don't struggle with or get fascinated by them. Have a sense of acceptance—even kindness—toward whatever passes through the open space of awareness.

Keep settling into the breath, perhaps with a growing sense of peacefulness. Be aware of the changing nature of what passes through the mind. Notice how it feels to get caught up in the passing contents of awareness—and how it feels to let them go by. Be aware of peaceful, spacious awareness itself.

When you like, bring the meditation to an end. Notice how you feel, and take in the good of your meditation.

FEELING SAFER

As we saw in chapter 2, the brain continually scans your inner and outer worlds for threats. When any are detected, your stress-response system fires up.

Occasionally, this vigilance is warranted, but usually it's excessive, driven by amygdala-hippocampus reactions to past events that are no longer likely. The anxiety that results is unnecessary and unpleasant, and it primes your brain and body to overreact to small things.

Additionally, vigilance and anxiety draw attention away from mindfulness and contemplative absorption. It's no accident that traditional instructions for meditation often encourage practitioners to find a place of seclusion where they are protected from harm. For example, the account of the Buddha's night of awakening has him sitting at the base of the Bodhi Tree, which "had his back." Feelings of safety tell the brain that it can afford to bring in the troops that have been manning the watchtowers, and put them to work internally to increase concentration and insight—or just let them get some rest.

But before we explore specific methods for feeling safer, two important points. First, in ordinary reality, there is no such thing as complete safety. Life is continually changing, cars run red lights, people get sick, and whole nations erupt and send shock waves around the world. There is no absolutely stable ground, no perfect shelter. Accepting this truth is wisdom, and embracing it and getting on with life can feel exhilarating. Second, for some people—especially those with a history of trauma—reducing anxiety can seem threatening, since lowering their guard makes them feel vulnerable. For these reasons, we speak of "safer" rather than "safe," and please adapt the methods that follow to your own needs.

Relax Your Body

Relaxation drains away anxiety like pulling the plug in a bathtub. (See the methods described earlier in this chapter.)

Use Imagery

Right hemisphere imagery is closely connected with emotional processing. To feel safer, visualize protective figures with you, such as a beloved grandmother or a guardian angel. Or imagine that you're surrounded by a bubble of light like a force field; in ticklish situations, I'll sometimes hear Captain Kirk's voice (from *Star Trek*) in my mind: "Shields up, Scotty!"

Connect with People Who Support You

Identify friends and family who care about you, and try to spend more time with them. When you're apart, visualize being with them and take in the good feelings. Companionship, even if only imagined, activates the brain's attachment and social group circuitry. Physical and emotional closeness to caregivers and other members of the band was a necessity for survival during our evolutionary history. Consequently, activating a felt sense of closeness will probably help you feel safer.

Bring Mindfulness to Fear

Anxiety, dread, apprehension, worry, and even panic are just mental states like any other. Recognize fear when it arises, observe the feeling of it in your body, watch it try to convince you that you should be alarmed, see it change and move on. Verbally describe to yourself what you're feeling, to increase frontal lobe regulation of the limbic system (Hariri, Bookheimer, and Mazziotta 2000; Lieberman et al. 2007). Notice how the awareness which contains fear is itself never fearful. Keep separating from the fear; settle back into the vast space of awareness through which fear passes like a cloud.

Evoke Inner Protectors

Enabled by the distributed network of the nervous system, different subpersonalities interact dynamically to form the seemingly monolithic but actually fragmented self. For example, one well-known threesome is called the inner child/critical parent/nurturing parent; a related triad is the victim/persecutor/protector. Your nurturing parent/protector subpersonality is reassuring, encouraging, and soothing, and it stands up against the inner and outer voices that are judgmental and demeaning. It does *not* flatter you or make things up. It is grounded in reality, like a solid, caring, no-nonsense teacher or coach who reminds you of good things about you and the world while telling mean people to back off and leave you alone.

Growing up, many of us felt let down by people who should have been better protectors. The deepest upsets are often not with those who harmed you but with the people who didn't prevent it—they're the ones you probably had the strongest attachment bonds to and thus felt most let down by. So it's understandable if your inner protector is not as strong as it could be. What you can do today is pay particular attention to the experience of being with strong people who care for you and stand up for you; savor this experience and take it in. Imagine, and perhaps write down, a conversation between an inner protector and a critical or alarming subpersonality, and make sure that the inner protector makes a powerful case for you.

Be Realistic

Draw on prefrontal capacities to evaluate: What is the chance that the feared event will happen? How bad would it be? How long would the damage last? What could I do to cope? Who could help me?

Most fears are exaggerated. As you go through life, your brain acquires expectations based on your experiences, particularly negative ones. When situations occur that are even remotely similar, your brain automatically applies its expectations to them; if it expects pain or loss, or even just the threat of these, it pulses fear signals. But because of the negativity bias, many expectations of pain or loss are overstated or completely unfounded.

For example, I was a shy child and considerably younger than most of the other kids in my classrooms, so I grew up feeling like an outsider, and a lonely one, in many situations. Later, as an adult, when I joined a new group (e.g., a team at work, the board of a nonprofit), I'd anticipate being an outsider again, and feel uncomfortable about it—even though the other people in the group were perfectly welcoming.

Expectations that come from childhood—often the most powerful ones of all—are particularly suspect. When you're young, (A) you have little choice about your family, school, and peers, (B) your parents and many others have much more power than you do, and (C) you don't have many resources yourself. But these days, the plain facts are that (A) you have many more choices about what you do in life, (B) power differentials between you and others are usually minimal or nonexistent, and (C) you have lots of inner and outer resources (e.g., coping skills, goodwill toward you from others). So, when a fear arises, ask yourself: "What options do I actually have? How could I exercise power skillfully to stick up for myself and take good care of myself? What resources could I draw upon?"

You're trying to see the world clearly, without distortion, confusion, or selective attention. What are the facts? Science, business, medicine, psychology, and contemplative practice are all founded on the truth of things, whatever it may be; in Buddhism, for example, ignorance is considered the fundamental source of suffering. Not surprisingly, studies have shown that appraising a situation more accurately leads to greater positive emotions and fewer negative ones (Gross and John 2003). And if there really is something to worry about, deal with it as best you can (e.g., pay the bill, see the doctor). Not only will doing *something* and moving forward feel better in its own right, it will also usually improve a situation that's worrying you (Aspinwall and Taylor 1997).

Nurture Your Sense of Secure Attachment

Your childhood relationships with major caregivers—notably your parents—have probably had a great influence on your expectations, attitudes, emotions, and actions in your important relationships as an adult. Dan Siegel (2001, 2007), Allan Schore (2003), Mary Main (Main, Hesse, and Kaplan 2005), and others have helped clarify the neurobiology of attachment. To summarize a large body of research, the recurring experiences a young child has with her parents—which are affected by the child's temperament—will lead to one of four modes of *attachment* to them: *secure, insecure-avoidant, insecure-anxious*, and *disorganized* (this last type is rare and won't be discussed further). The type of attachment to one parent is largely independent of the type of attachment to the other one. Insecure attachment modes appear to be associated with characteristic patterns of neural activity, such as a lack of integration between the prefrontal cortex (PFC) and the limbic system (Siegel 2001).

Attachment modes tend to persist into adulthood and become the underlying, default template for important relationships. If, like a large fraction of the population, you grew up with insecure-avoidant or insecure-anxious attachment, you can still change that template so you experience a greater sense of security in your relationships. Here are some good methods for doing so:

- Develop self-understanding of how your upbringing affected your relationships with your parents, especially in early childhood; acknowledge any insecure attachment.

- Bring compassion to yourself for any sense of insecurity.

- As much as possible, seek out nurturing and reliable people, and take in the feeling of being with them. Also do what you can to be treated well in your existing relationships.

- Practice mindfulness of your inner state, including through meditation. In effect, you are giving yourself today the attention and attunement you should have received as a child. Mindfulness activates the mid-line regions of your brain and helps increase the coordination between the PFC and the limbic system; these are key neural substrates of secure attachment (Siegel 2007).

FINDING REFUGE

In this life, where have you found refuge? Refuges include people, places, memories, ideas, and ideals—anyone or anything that provides reliable sanctuary and protection, so you can let down your guard and gather strength and wisdom. As a child, refuge might have been your mother's lap, reading in bed, or hanging out with friends. Personally, I spent a lot of time in the hills around my home, clearing my head and getting refueled by nature.

Today as an adult, your refuge might be a particular location or activity (e.g., a church or temple, a quiet walk with your dog, a long bath) or the company of your mate, good friends, or perhaps a teacher. Some refuges are ineffable, though potentially more profound: confidence in the power of reason, feeling connected with nature, or a basic intuition of the fundamental alrightness of all things.

Consider these refuges, adapted from Buddhism with some broadened meanings:

- Teacher—the historical figure at the center of a faith tradition (such as Jesus, Moses, Siddhartha, or Mohammed) in whom one has confidence; qualities embodied by that person which are also present within you

- Truth—reality itself and accurate descriptions of it (e.g., how suffering arises and ends)

- Good company—both those who are farther along on the path of awakening and those joined with you in fellowship near at hand

Taking refuge pulls you away from reactivating situations and concerns, and then fills you with positive influences. As you rest increasingly in a background sense of refuge, neurons are quietly stitching a safety net for you. On the path of awakening, it's natural to experience some upheaval, dark nights of the soul, or unnerving groundlessness when the foundation of old beliefs falls away. At these times, your refuges will catch you and help you ride out the storm.

Try to take refuge in one or more things every day. This can be formal or informal, verbal or nonverbal—whatever works best for you. Experiment with different ways to experience refuge, such as the sense that the refuge is where you come from or that it flows through you.

Exploring Your Refuges

Identify several of your refuges. Then apply this exploration to as many of them as you like. You can do this with your eyes open or closed, slowly or quickly. Instead of the suggested phrase, *I find refuge in _____,* you could try:

I take refuge in _____.

I go for refuge to _____.

I abide as _____.

I come from _____.

There is _____ here.

_____ flows through me.

I am one with _____.

Or whatever you like.

Bring to mind a refuge. Get a feeling or idea of it, and sense it in your body. Get a sense of how it's wholesome for you to take refuge there. To have its influence in your life. To come from that place. To have its shelter and protection.

Say softly in your mind: I find refuge in _____. *Or wordlessly feel yourself entering refuge there.*

Notice how it feels to have entered this refuge. Let that feeling sink in and become a part of you.

When you like, move on to the next refuge. And then to as many refuges as you want.

When you are finished entering your refuges, notice what the experience as a whole feels like. Know that as you go through your days, you'll carry your refuges with you.

chapter 5: KEY POINTS

🪷 The most powerful way to use the mind-body connection to improve your physical and mental health is through guiding your autonomic nervous system (ANS). Every time you calm the ANS through stimulating the parasympathetic nervous system (PNS), you tilt your body, brain, and mind increasingly toward inner peace and well-being.

🪷 You can activate the PNS in many ways, including relaxation, big exhalations, touching the lips, mindfulness of the body, imagery, balancing your heartbeat, and meditation.

🪷 Meditation increases gray matter in brain regions that handle attention, compassion, and empathy. It also helps a variety of medical conditions, strengthens the immune system, and improves psychological functioning.

🪷 Deliberately feeling safer helps control the hardwired tendency to look for and overreact to threats. Feel safer by relaxing, using imagery, connecting with others, being mindful of fear itself, evoking inner protectors, being realistic, and increasing your sense of secure attachment.

🪷 Find refuge in whatever is a sanctuary and refueling station for you. Potential refuges include people, activities, places, and intangible things like reason, a sense of your innermost being, or truth.

chapter 6

Strong Intentions

Do all that you can, with all that you have, in the time
that you have, in the place where you are.

—Nkosi Johnson

The previous chapter focused on cooling down greed and hatred to reduce the causes of suffering. This chapter is about "warming up" the inner strength that will increase the causes of your happiness. You'll see how your brain gets motivated—how it establishes intentions and pursues them—and how to use these neural networks to move forward strongly in the days to come. To be alive is to lean into the future (Thompson 2007), to stretch for the next breath or meal. Or reach for happiness, love, and wisdom.

THE NEUROAXIS

Your brain evolved from the bottom up and the inside out, along what is called the *neuroaxis* (Lewis and Todd 2007; Tucker, Derryberry, and Luv 2000), which is one way to conceptualize the organization of the brain. Starting at the base, let's explore how each of the four main levels of the neuroaxis supports your intentions.

Brain Stem

The brain stem sends neuromodulators such as norepinephrine and dopamine throughout your brain in order to get you ready for action, keep you energized while you pursue your goals, and reward you when you attain them.

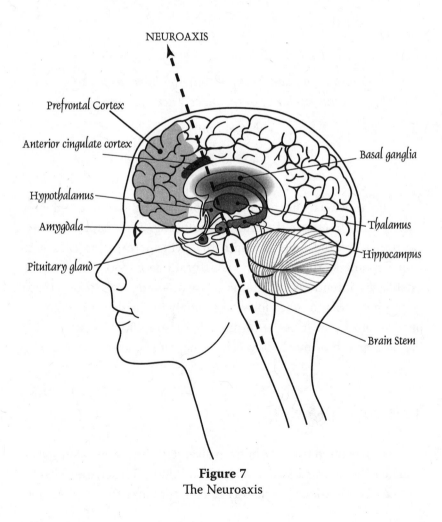

Figure 7
The Neuroaxis

Diencephalon

The *diencephalon* consists of the thalamus (the brain's central switchboard for sensory information) and the hypothalamus, which directs your autonomic nervous system and influences your endocrine system through the pituitary gland. The hypothalamus regulates primal drive states (e.g., for water, food, sex) and primal emotions (e.g., terror, rage).

Limbic System

The limbic system evolved from the diencephalon, and includes the amygdala, hippocampus, and basal ganglia. It's basically Grand Central Station for emotion.

Limbic structures lie to the sides of the diencephalon, and in some cases beneath it (e.g., amygdala). They are considered a higher level in the neuroaxis since they are more recent in evolution—even though some of these structures are lower down, which can be a little confusing.

Cortex

The cortex includes the prefrontal cortex (PFC), cingulate, and insula. These regions—which play a prominent role in this book—handle abstract reasoning and concepts, values, planning, and the "executive functions" of organization, self-monitoring, and impulse control. The cortex also includes the sensory and motor strips that stretch more or less from ear to ear (sensation and movement), the parietal lobes (perception), the temporal lobes (language and memory), and the occipital lobe (vision).

These four levels work together to keep you motivated; they're integrated up and down the neuroaxis. In general, the lower levels orient and energize the upper ones, which guide and inhibit the lower ones. The lower levels have more direct control over your body and less capacity to change their own neural networks. The upper levels are the opposite: although they're more removed from the action, they have vastly greater neuroplasticity—the capacity to be shaped by neural/mental activity, to learn from experience. At all levels of the neuroaxis, the intentions—the goals and related strategies—at work in your life operate mainly outside of your awareness.

The farther down the neuroaxis, the more immediate the reactions; higher up on the neuroaxis, time frames stretch. For example, cortical influences help you pass up a reward right now in order to gain a greater one in the future (McClure et al. 2004). Usually, the longer the view, the wiser the intentions.

THE MOTIVATIONAL MACROSYSTEM

The Anterior Cingulate Cortex Hub

Although each part of the neuroaxis works with the others, two regions in particular are hubs, sending out neural spokes in many directions: the anterior cingulate cortex (ACC) and the amygdala. Let's start with the ACC (for more details, see Lewis and Todd, 2007; Paus 2001).

The ACC is closely connected to the evolutionarily recent *dorsal* (upper) and *lateral* (outer) regions of the prefrontal cortex, known by the mouth-watering acronym DLPFC. The DLPFC is a key neural *substrate*, or basis, of *working memory*, which is a kind of workspace where your brain gathers information to solve problems and make decisions. The ACC is also closely connected to the supplementary motor area, where new actions are planned. Through these links, your ACC guides your actions to fulfill your intentions.

When an intention crystallizes, your inner experience of things coming together toward a unified aim reflects a *neural coherence*. In the cortical "spokes" of the ACC, many far-flung (on the microscopic scale of cells) regions start pulsing together, matching the phases—

the highs and lows—of their firing rhythms, typically in the gamma range of neural synchrony: 30 to 80 times a second (Thompson and Varela 2001).

The ACC is the primary overseer of your attention. It monitors progress toward your goals, and flags any conflicts among them. Its upper layers manage *effortful control*, the deliberate and sustained regulation of thoughts and behavior. These areas don't fully develop until ages three to six (Posner and Rothbart 2000), a major reason why young children have less self-control than older ones. Any time you consciously exercise your will, your ACC is involved.

Through its dense, reciprocal connections to the amygdala, hippocampus, and hypothalamus, the ACC influences your emotions and is influenced by them as well. Therefore, it's a key site for the integration of thinking and feeling (Lewis 2005). Strengthening the ACC—such as through meditation—helps you think clearly when you're upset, and brings warmth and emotional intelligence to your logical reasoning.

In sum, the ACC is at the center of top-down, deliberate, centralized, reasoned motivation.

The Amygdala Hub

Through its own dense connections to the ACC, PFC, hippocampus, hypothalamus, basal ganglia, and brain stem, the amygdala is the second major hub of motivational activity.

Moment to moment, the amygdala spotlights what's relevant and important to you: what's pleasant and unpleasant, what's an opportunity and what's a threat. It also shapes and shades your perceptions, appraisals of situations, attributions of intentions to others, and judgments. It exerts these influences largely outside of your awareness, which increases their power since they operate out of sight.

When you get motivated in any significant way, it means the subcortical regions that connect to the amygdala have synchronized with each other. The neural networks in the limbic system, hypothalamus, and brain stem start pulsing together, usually in the theta frequency of four to seven times a second (Kocsis and Vertes 1994; Lewis 2005).

In sum, the amygdala is at the center of bottom-up, reactive, distributed, passionate motivation.

Head and Heart

Together, the ACC and amygdala hubs form a joint system that's involved in just about every aspect of motivated activity. These hubs modulate each other; for example, in a three-step feedback loop, the amygdala excites the lower parts of your ACC, which then excite its upper parts, which in turn inhibit the amygdala (Lewis and Todd 2007). Consequently, the ostensibly rational ACC-based network is deeply involved in your emotions and drives through its downward projections into the three lower levels of the neuroaxis. Meanwhile, the supposedly irrational amygdala-based network helps construct your appraisals, values, and strategies through its upward projections into the cortex.

This integration can happen within a fraction of a second, as neural populations all along the neuroaxis synchronize with each other in response to motivationally meaningful information, phase-locking their rhythms together. In a more general way, such integration can continue for many years. Consider how your "cool" ACC-based and "warm" amygdala-based motivations have worked together in the important areas of your life. For example, warm-hearted advocacy for a child with special needs benefits from cool clarity about how to keep working with a school district to get the most resources for her.

On the other hand, these two hubs can also be out of step or tug against each other. For example, during adolescence, the amygdala-based network often overpowers the ACC-based network. In terms of your own motivations, are your ACC- and amygdala-based networks equally strong? And are they—head and heart, metaphorically speaking—pulling in the same direction? For example, I realized some years ago that the training of my head had gotten out in front of the cultivation of my heart, so I've been focusing more on the latter ever since.

Intentions and Suffering

It is sometimes said that desire leads to suffering, but is that always true? The territory of desire is far-reaching, and it includes wishes, intentions, hopes, and cravings. Whether a desire leads to suffering depends on two factors: Is craving—the sense that you need something—involved? And what is the desire *for*? Regarding the first of these, desire per se is not the root of suffering; craving is. You can wish for or intend something without craving the results; for example, you can decide to get eggs from the refrigerator without craving them—and without getting upset if there are none left.

Regarding the second factor, intentions are a double-edged sword that can either hurt or help. For example, the Three Poisons—greed, hatred, and delusion—are a kind of intention: to grab pleasure and hold on tight, resist pain and anything else you don't like, and ignore or distort things you'd rather not know about.

Harmful intentions operate at all levels of the brain, from rage and fear released by the hypothalamus to subtle plans for payback constructed by the PFC. But the same is also true of wholesome inclinations toward generosity, kindness, and insight: they ripple up and down the neuroaxis, from visceral brain stem energy for good causes to abstract ideals sustained by the PFC. As you weave positive inclinations more deeply into the different levels of your brain, you increasingly push the Three Poisons to the margins. It's important to nurture good intentions at *all* levels of the neuroaxis—and to cultivate the strength to carry them out.

FEELING STRONG

During a break from college, I helped take a dozen school kids back-packing through the Yosemite high country. We didn't see anyone all day before stopping for lunch at a rocky area by a river, where the trail disappeared. Then we headed into the forest, where we picked up the trail again. A mile or so later, one of the kids realized he'd left his jacket back by the river. I said I'd go get it and meet the group at our campground several miles ahead. Dropping my pack by the side of the trail, I returned to our lunch area, searched around, and found the jacket.

But now I couldn't find the trail. After casting about for a while amidst the jumbled boulders, it really hit me: it was late afternoon, the only people around were miles away, it was already getting chilly, and I was looking at spending the night at 6,000 feet in a T-shirt and jeans. Then an unprecedented and powerful sense came over me. I felt like a feral animal, like a hawk that would do whatever it takes to survive. I felt a fierce determination to live through the day and, if need be, the night. Newly energized, I scrambled in widening circles, finally finding the trail. I made it to our campsite later that night. I've never forgotten the intense feelings of that day, and have drawn on them for strength many times since.

When have you felt really strong yourself? What was that experience like—in your body, your emotions, and your thoughts? Strength is often quiet, receptive determination rather than chest-thumping pushiness. One of the strongest people I've ever known was my mother, who just kept taking care of her family no matter what.

Feeling Stronger

Strength has two primary aspects: energy and determination. You can intensify these by quickening your breathing a little, or by tightening your shoulders slightly, as if you're bracing to carry a load. Get familiar with the muscle movements—often subtle ones—

associated with strength. Just as making the facial expression of an emotion will heighten that feeling (Niedenthal 2007), engaging the muscle movements of strength will increase your experience of it.

Get in the habit of deliberately calling up a sense of strength—not to dominate anybody or anything, but to fuel your intentions (see the exercise, "Many Ways to Feel Strong"). Involve the entire neuroaxis in order to power up your experience of strength. For example, bring to mind a sense of visceral, muscular willfulness to stimulate your brain stem to send norepinephrine and dopamine like a rising fountain up into the rest of your brain for arousal and drive. Bring the limbic system into the action by focusing on how good it feels to be strong, so you'll be increasingly drawn to strength in the future. Add the power of cortical language by commenting on the experience to yourself: *I'm feeling strong. It's good to be strong.* Notice any beliefs that it's bad or wrong to be strong, and send them on their way with counterthoughts like *Strength helps me do good things. I have the right to be strong.* Make sure that the intentions at all levels of your neuroaxis are heading in the same direction.

When you experience strength—whether you evoked it deliberately or it just came to mind—consciously take it in so it deepens its traces in implicit memory and becomes a part of you.

Many Ways to Feel Strong

There are many ways to find and intensify the feeling of strength. This exercise explores some of them; feel free to adapt it however you like. It's best to keep your eyes open during it, since you'll want strength in everyday situations in which your eyes are open.

Take a breath and come into yourself. Be aware of thoughts passing through your mind without any need to engage with them. Feel the strength in awareness, always clear and everlasting, no matter what passes through it.

Now sense the vitality in your body. Notice how your breathing has a strength of its own. Sense your muscles, your capacity to move in any direction. Sense the animal strength in your body (even if it is also weak in some ways).

Recall a time when you felt really strong. Imagine that situation as intensely as you can. Bring to mind the sense of strength you experienced. Strength in your breathing, energy in your arms and legs. That same strength is beating today in your powerful heart. Whatever you feel is fine. And continue to open to the sense that you are strong, clear, and determined. Notice how it feels good to feel strong. Let strength sink into your being. (If you like, recall additional times you felt strong.)

Now, continuing to feel strong, bring to mind a person (or group of people) who supports you. Make this as real as possible; imagine this person's face, the sound of his or her voice. Let yourself feel supported, valued, believed in. Sense how this feeling of support increases your sense of strength. Notice how it feels good to feel strong. Let strength sink into your being. (You can repeat this for other people who support you.)

Notice any other feelings coming up, too—perhaps even opposite ones like weakness. Whatever is arising is fine. Just notice it, let it be, and let it go. Turn your attention back to your sense of being strong.

Finally, abiding in a sense of strength, bring to awareness a challenging situation. Solid in your strength, feel a spaciousness around that difficult condition. Allow it to be what it is while you continue to feel strong and centered. Be strong, with no need to grasp or struggle in any way. Any problems are flowing through awareness like clouds across the sky. Be spacious, relaxed, and easy. Feel the strength, in your breathing, in your awareness, in the clarity of your mind, in the wholeness of your body, in your good intentions.

As you go through your day, pay attention to the sense of feeling strong. Notice how it feels good to feel strong. Let strength sink into your being.

chapter 6: KEY POINTS

🌼 It's important both to cool the causes of suffering and to warm up the causes of happiness—such as your intentions. Intentions involve strength applied to clear and appropriate goals, sustained over time. Most of the intentions operating in your brain do so outside of awareness.

🌼 To simplify, your brain evolved in four levels, along a kind of neuroaxis; these levels work together to keep you motivated. From the bottom up, along the neuroaxis, they are the brain stem, diencephalon, limbic system, and cortex.

🌼 In general, the farther down the neuroaxis a response takes place, the faster, more intense, and more automatic it is. Higher on the neuroaxis, responses become more delayed, less intense, and more considered. In particular, the cortex—the most evolutionarily recent level—really enhances your capacity to take the future into account. Usually, the longer the view, the wiser the intentions.

🌼 The neuroaxis has two hubs: the anterior cingulate cortex (ACC) and the amygdala. The ACC-based network manages top-down, deliberate, centralized, reasoned motivation, while the amygdala-based network handles bottom-up, reactive, distributed, passionate motivation.

🌼 These two networks are woven together. For example, the "logical" ACC-based network guides the flow of your feelings, and the "emotional" amygdala-based network shapes your values and worldview.

❀ The two networks—metaphorically the head and the heart—can support each other, be awkwardly out of sync, or struggle in outright conflict. Ideally, your intentions will be aligned with each other at all levels of the neuroaxis: that's when they have the most power.

❀ Intentions are a form of desire. Desire per se is not the root of suffering; craving is. The key is to have wholesome intentions without being attached to their results.

❀ Inner strength comes in many forms, including quiet perseverance. Get familiar with what strength feels like in your body so you can call it up again. Deliberately stimulate feelings of strength to deepen their neural pathways.

chapter 7

Equanimity

Equanimity is a perfect, unshakable balance of mind.
—Nyanaponika Thera

Imagine that your mind is like a house with a mud-room—the entry room in cold climates where people put their messy boots and dripping coats. With *equanimity,* your initial reactions to things—reach for this carrot, push away that stick—are left in a mental mud-room so that the interior of your mind remains clear and clean and peaceful.

The word equanimity comes from Latin roots meaning "even" and "mind." With equanimity, what passes through your mind is held with spaciousness so you stay even-keeled and aren't thrown off balance. The ancient circuitry of the brain is continually driving you to react one way or another—and equanimity is your circuit breaker. Equanimity breaks the chain of suffering by separating the feeling tones of experience from the machinery of craving, neutralizing your reactions to those feeling tones.

For example, one time I came home from a meditation retreat, we sat down to dinner, and soon our kids were doing their usual bickering. Normally this would have bothered me, but because of the equanimity gained from the retreat, the irritation in my mind was like an annoying fan yelling from the upper bleachers in a stadium far above me, while I was down below and not hijacked by it. Psychologists have a term—*demand characteristics*—for the aspects of situations that really pull at you, like a doorbell ringing or someone reaching out his hand to shake yours. With equanimity, situations have only characteristics, not demands.

Equanimity is neither apathy nor indifference: you are warmly engaged with the world but not troubled by it. Through its nonreactivity, it creates a great space for compassion, loving-kindness, and joy at the good fortune of others. For example, the Buddhist teacher Kamala Masters tells the story of taking a boat down the Ganges at dawn. On her left, the sun lit ancient towers and temples with an exquisite rosy glow. On her right, funeral pyres were burning, and the sounds of wailing rose up with the smoke. Beauty to the left and death to the right, with equanimity opening her heart wide enough to include both. You draw on this same equanimity to stay centered and large-hearted when you face situations that have great personal impact, such as when you—or a dear friend—lose a loved one.

A Taste of Equanimity

If you like, take some time here to get a taste of equanimity. It won't be the all-encompassing sense that is available in the deepest meditations, but it will give you a feeling for the evenness, clarity, and peacefulness of this state of mind.

Relax. Take a few minutes to steady your mind by focusing on the sensations of breathing in your belly or chest, or around your upper lip.

Become increasingly mindful of the changing feeling tones—pleasant, unpleasant, or neutral—of your experience.

Sense a growing impartiality toward whatever arises, an ease, a relaxed and undisturbed presence. Accept and be at peace with whatever is arising. Let your mind become increasingly steady, quiet, and collected.

Be aware of sounds. Hear without being caught by what's heard. Be aware of sensations. Sense without being caught by what's sensed. Be aware of thoughts. Think without being caught by what's thought.

Notice how pleasant, unpleasant, and neutral feeling tones come and go. They're constantly changing, and not a dependable basis for happiness.

Be aware of passing thoughts and feelings without identifying with them. No one needs to own them.

Be aware of passing thoughts and feelings without reacting to them. Notice a growing disengagement. There's less tilting toward pleasure, less pulling back from pain.

In the pleasant, there is just the pleasant, with no reactions added. In the unpleasant, there is just the unpleasant, with no reactions added. In the neutral, there is just the neutral, with no reactions added. This is the mind of no preferences. Rest as awareness, free from reactions.

Abide as equanimity. Breath after breath. At ease. Settle into deeper and deeper layers of equanimity. As you can, sense a sublime freedom, contentment, and peace.

If they aren't already open, open your eyes. Bring visual sensations into your equanimity. Explore the mind of no preferences for whatever crosses your gaze, be it pleasant, unpleasant, or neutral. Move your body a bit as you finish the meditation. Explore the mind of no preferences for body sensations, be they pleasant, unpleasant, or neutral.

As your day proceeds, notice what it's like to bring more equanimity to people and situations.

THE EQUANIMOUS BRAIN

When you are equanimous, you don't grasp after enjoyable experiences or push against disagreeable ones. Rather, you have a kind of space around experiences—a buffer between you and their feeling tones. This state of being is not based on standard prefrontal control of emotions, in which there is inhibition and direction of limbic activity. Instead, with equanimity, the limbic system can fire however it "wants." The primary point of equanimity is not to reduce or channel that activation, but *simply not to respond to it.* This is very unusual behavior for the brain, which is designed by evolution to respond to limbic signals, particularly to pulses of pleasant and unpleasant feeling tones. What could be happening, neurologically, to accomplish this? Let's look at the different aspects of equanimity and the parts of the brain they likely involve.

Understanding and Intention

With equanimity, you see into the transient and imperfect nature of experience, and your aim is to remain *disenchanted*—free of the spells cast by pleasure and pain. In this—rather Buddhist— sense of the word, disenchanted, you are not disappointed or dissatisfied with life; you simply see through its apparent charms and alarms and are not knocked off center by either.

Understanding and intention are both grounded in the prefrontal cortex. The intention to remain equanimous relies in particular on the anterior cingulate cortex (ACC) hub in the neuroaxis.

Great Steadiness of Mind

Equanimity also involves remaining aware of the passing stream without letting any bit of it hook you. This entails anterior cingulate oversight, especially in the beginning stages of equanimity. As equanimity deepens, meditators report an effortless continuity of mindfulness, which presumably correlates with reduced ACC activity and self-organizing stability in the neural substrates of awareness.

A Global Workspace of Consciousness

Another aspect of equanimity is an unusually expansive *global workspace of consciousness* (Baars 1997), the neural complement to the mental sense of great spaciousness surrounding the objects of awareness. This could be enabled by stable and far-reaching gamma-wave synchronization of billions of neurons across large areas of the brain, rhythmically firing together 30–80 times a second. Interestingly, this atypical brainwave pattern is seen in Tibetan monks with lots of meditation practice—and a lot of equanimity (Lutz et al. 2004).

Dampening the Stress-Response System

The limbic, HPAA, and sympathetic nervous systems react to each other in circular ways. For example, if something frightening occurs, your body will tend to become activated (e.g., increased heart rate, sweaty palms); those bodily changes will be interpreted by the limbic system as evidence of a threat, which will trigger more fear reactions in a vicious cycle. Through activating the parasympathetic nervous system (PNS), you prevent the stress-response system from reacting to its own reactions. This is one reason why the training for equanimity in contemplative settings involves considerable relaxation and tranquility.

The Fruits of Equanimity

Over time, equanimity deepens into a profound inner stillness that is a defining characteristic of contemplative absorption (Brahm 2006). It also becomes increasingly woven into daily life, bringing great benefit. If you can break the link between feeling tones and craving—if you can be

With equanimity, you can deal with situations with calm and reason while keeping your inner happiness.
—The Dalai Lama

with the pleasant without chasing after it, with the unpleasant without resisting it, and with the neutral without ignoring it—then you have cut the chain of suffering, at least for a time. And that is an incredible blessing and freedom.

DEVELOPING THE FACTORS OF EQUANIMITY

While complete equanimity is an uncommon state for both the mind and the brain, a basic sense of it can be experienced in everyday life and developed with practice. The underlying neural factors we've explored suggest a number of ways to encourage this process.

Understanding

Recognize the fleeting nature of rewards and that they usually aren't actually all that great. See, too, that painful experiences are transient and usually not that awful. Neither pleasure nor pain is worth claiming as your own or identifying with. Further, consider how every event is determined by countless preceding factors so that things can not be any other way. This is not fatalism or despair: you can take action to make the *future* different. But even then, remember that most of the factors that shape the future are out of your hands. You can do everything right, and still the glass will break, the project will go nowhere, you'll catch the flu, or a friend will remain upset.

I make myself rich by making my wants few.
—Henry David Thoreau

Intention

Keep reminding yourself of the important reasons for equanimity: you want more freedom from craving and the suffering it brings.

Routinely recall your intention to be aware of the feeling tone, to be spacious around it, and to let it be whatever it is without reacting to it. To help hold this in mind, put a little sticky note with "equanimity" on it near your computer or telephone, or use a picture of a beautiful, tranquil setting.

Steadiness of Mind

Chapters 11 and 12 will explore various ways to cultivate an increasingly stable presence of mind. As your mind grows steadier, pay particular attention to the neutral feeling tone. Stimuli that evoke a pleasant or unpleasant feeling tone stir up more brain activity than neutral tones do, because there is more to think about and respond to. Since your brain doesn't naturally stay engaged with neutral stimuli, you must make a conscious effort to sustain attention to them. Through sensitizing yourself to the neutral aspects of experience, your mind will become more comfortable staying with them, and less inclined to seek rewards or scan for threats. In time, the neutral tone can become, as my teacher Christina Feldman puts it, a "doorway to the eventless"—an entry into the stillness of the ground of being, which never changes and is always the same.

Spacious Awareness

Imagine the contents of your mind coming and going in a vast open space of awareness, like shooting stars. The feeling tones of experience are just more contents moving through this space. Boundless space surrounds them—dwarfing them, untroubled by them, unaffected by their passing. The space of awareness allows every content of mind to be or not to be, to come and to go. Thoughts are just thoughts, sounds are just sounds, situations are just situations, and people are just being themselves. As Ajahn Sumedho said during a talk at Chithurst Monastery, "Trust in awareness, in being awake, rather than in transient and unstable conditions" (2006).

Tranquility

This involves not acting based on the feeling tone. For example, you don't automatically move toward something just because it is pleasant. In the words of the Third Zen Patriarch: "The Great Way is not difficult for those who have no preferences" (Kornfield 1996, 143). Set aside a period of your day—even just a minute long—to consciously release preferences for or against anything. Then extend this practice to more and more of your day. Your actions will be guided increasingly by your values and virtues, not by desires that are reactions to positive or negative feeling tones.

Tranquility involves parasympathetic activation, which you've learned how to encourage in chapter 5. Make a list of situations that trigger strong greed or hatred (broadly defined) in you, arranged from mild triggers all the way up to your equivalent of a four-alarm fire. Then, starting with the easier situations and working your way up the list, deliberately focus on bringing greater tranquility to them by using some of chapter 5's approaches, such as big exhalations, being mindful of the fear, or taking refuge.

Inner peace can definitely be sustained in difficult circumstances. Here are two examples that are worlds apart, yet have aspects of equanimity in common:

Think of Joe Montana playing football, guiding the 49ers downfield while 300-pound defensive linemen rushed to crush him to the ground. His teammates said that the crazier and more desperate the game got, the cooler Joe became. My wife and I used to joke: *Three minutes left in the fourth quarter of the Super Bowl, eighty yards to go for the game-winning touchdown—Joe's got them right where he wants them!*

And consider Ramana Maharshi, the great Indian saint who passed away in 1950. Toward the end of his life, he developed cancer in his arm. Although this must have been very painful, he remained serene and loving throughout his final days. One time he looked down with a beautiful smile and said simply, "Poor arm."

Buddhism has a metaphor for the different conditions in life. They're called the Eight Worldly Winds: pleasure and pain, praise and blame, gain and loss, fame and ill repute. As you develop greater equanimity, these winds have less effect on your mind. Your happiness becomes increasingly unconditional, not based on catching a good breeze instead of a bad one.

chapter 7: KEY POINTS

- Equanimity means not reacting to your reactions, whatever they are.

- Equanimity creates a buffer around the feeling tones of experiences so that you do not react to them with craving. Equanimity is like a circuit breaker that blocks the normal sequence in the mind that moves from feeling tone to craving to clinging to suffering.

- Equanimity is not coldness, indifference, or apathy. You are present in the world but not upset by it. The spaciousness of equanimity is a great support for compassion, kindness, and joy at the happiness of others.

- In daily life and meditation, deepen your equanimity by becoming increasingly mindful of the feeling tones of experience and increasingly disenchanted with them. They come and they go, and they're not worth chasing or resisting.

- Equanimity is an unusual brain state. It is not based on prefrontal inhibition of the limbic system. Rather, it involves not reacting to the limbic system. This probably draws on four neural conditions: prefrontal and anterior cingular cortex (ACC) activation for understanding and intention; steadiness of mind, driven initially by ACC oversight but then self-organizing; fast gamma-wave entrainment of large areas of the brain to create the mental experience of great spaciousness; and parasympathetic activation to dampen limbic/SNS/HPAA feedback loops that would otherwise make the stress-response system react to its own reactions in vicious cycles.

🪷 You can strengthen the neural factors of equanimity with the methods summarized in this chapter and discussed in greater detail throughout this book. As you do this, your happiness will become increasingly unconditional and unshakeable.

Part Three

Love

chapter 8

Two Wolves in the Heart

*All sentient beings developed through natural selection
in such a way that pleasant sensations serve as their
guide, and especially the pleasure derived from
sociability and from loving our families.*

—Charles Darwin

I heard a story once about a Native American elder who was asked
how she had become so wise, so happy, and so respected. She
answered: "In my heart, there are two wolves: a wolf of love and a
wolf of hate. It all depends on which one I feed each day."

This story always gives me a little shiver. It's both humbling and
hopeful. First, the wolf of love is very popular, but who among us
does not also harbor a wolf of hate? We can hear its snarling both
far away in distant wars and close to home in our own anger and
aggression, even toward people we love. Second, the story suggests
that we each have the ability—grounded in daily actions—to encourage and strengthen empathy, compassion, and kindness while also
restraining and reducing ill will, disdain, and aggression.

What are these wolves and where did they come from? And how can we feed the wolf of love and starve the wolf of hate? This chapter considers the first question; the next two chapters explore the second.

THE EVOLUTION OF RELATIONSHIP

Although the wolf of hate gets more headlines, the wolf of love has been painstakingly bred by evolution to be more powerful—and more central to your deepest nature. In the long march from tiny sponges in the ancient seas to humanity today, relating well to other members of one's species has been a great aid to survival. During the past 150-million-year journey of animal evolution, the advantages of social abilities were arguably the most influential factor driving the development of the brain. There were three major advances, and you benefit from them every day.

Vertebrates

The first proto-mammals probably lived about 180 million years ago, followed by the earliest birds around 30 million years later (these dates are approximate because of the ambiguous fossil record). Mammals and birds face survival challenges similar to those of reptiles and fish—harsh habitats and hungry predators—yet in proportion to body weight, mammals and birds have bigger brains. Why?

Reptiles and fish usually don't take care of their young—and may in fact eat them!—and typically make their way in life without a partner. By contrast, mammals and birds raise their young, and in many cases, they form pair bonds, sometimes for life.

In the dry language of evolutionary neuroscience, the "computational requirements" of selecting a good mate, sharing food, and keeping young alive required increased neural processing in mammals and birds (Dunbar and Shultz 2007). A squirrel or sparrow has to be smarter than a lizard or shark: better able to plan, communicate, cooperate, and negotiate. These are the exact skills that human couples discover are critical when they become parents, especially if they want to remain mates.

Primates

The next major step in brain evolution occurred with the primates that first appeared roughly 80 million years ago. Their defining characteristic was and is great sociability. For example, monkeys and apes spend up to a sixth of their day grooming other members of their troop. Interestingly, in one species studied—Barbary macaques—the groomers experienced more stress relief than the groomees (Shutt et al. 2007). (I've tried to use this rationale to get more back scratches from my wife, but so far she's not buying it.) The evolutionary bottom line is that, for both female and male primates, social success—which reflects relationship skills—leads to more offspring (Silk 2007).

In fact, the more sociable a primate species is—measured by things like breeding group size, number of grooming partners, and complexity of hierarchies—the bigger its cortex is compared to the rest of the brain (Dunbar and Shultz 2007; Sapolsky 2006). More-complex relationships require more-complex brains.

Further, only the great apes—the most modern family of primates, which includes chimpanzees, gorillas, orangutans, and humans—have developed *spindle cells*, a remarkable type of neuron that supports advanced social capabilities (Allman et al. 2001; Nimchinsky et al. 1999). For example, great apes routinely console other members of their troop who are upset, although this type of behavior is rare among other primates (de Waal 2006). Like us, chimpanzees laugh and cry (Bard 2006).

Spindle cells are found only in the cingulate cortex and insula, indicating that these regions—and their functions of empathy and self-awareness—have experienced intense evolutionary pressure over the last several million years (Allman et al. 2001; Nimchinsky et al.

1999). In other words, the benefits of relationships helped drive the recent evolution of the primate brain.

Humans

About 2.6 million years ago our hominid ancestors began making stone tools (Semaw et al. 1997). Since then the brain has tripled in size, even though it uses roughly ten times as many metabolic resources as an equivalent amount of muscle (Dunbar and Shultz 2007). This enlargement has challenged the female body to evolve, as well, in order to enable babies with bigger brains to exit the birth canal (Simpson et al. 2008). Given its biological costs, this rapid growth must have conferred great survival benefits—and most of what's been added is used for social, emotional, linguistic, and conceptual processing (Balter 2007). For example, humans have many more spindle neurons than the other great apes; these create a kind of information superhighway running from the cingulate cortex and the insula—two regions that are crucial to social and emotional intelligence—to other parts of your brain (Allman et al. 2001). Although an adult chimpanzee is better than a two-year-old child at figuring out the physical world, that young human is already much smarter about relationships (Herrmann et al. 2007).

This process of neural evolution may seem dry and remote, but it played out in the daily life-and-death struggles of beings like us in many ways. For millions of years, until the advent of agriculture about 10,000 years ago, our ancestors lived in hunter-gatherer bands, usually with fewer than 150 members (Norenzayan and Shariff 2008). They bred mainly within their own band while searching for food, avoiding predators, and competing with other bands for scarce resources. In that harsh environment, individuals who cooperated with other members of their band typically lived longer and left more offspring (Wilson 1999). Further, bands with strong teamwork usually beat bands with weak teamwork at getting resources, surviving, and passing on their genes (Nowak 2006).

Even small reproductive advantages in a single generation accumulate significantly over time (Bowles 2006), much the way small differences in team batting averages add up over the course of a long baseball season. Over the 100,000 generations since tools were first invented, those genes that fostered relationship abilities and cooperative tendencies pushed their way forward in the human gene pool. We see the results today in the neural underpinnings of many essential features of human nature, including altruism (Bowles 2006; Judson 2007), generosity (Harbaugh, Mayr, and Burghart 2007; Moll et al. 2006; Rilling et al. 2002), concern about reputation (Bateson, Nettle, and Robert 2006), fairness (de Quervain et al. 2004; Singer et al. 2006), language (Cheney and Seyfarth 2008), forgiveness (Nowak 2006), and morality and religion (Norenzayan and Shariff 2008).

CIRCUITS OF EMPATHY

Powerful evolutionary processes have shaped your nervous system to produce the capabilities and inclinations that foster cooperative relationships; they've nourished a large and friendly wolf in your heart. Building on this general sociability, related neural networks support *empathy*, the capacity to sense the inner state of another person, which is required for any kind of real closeness. If there were no empathy, we'd make our way in life like ants or bees, brushing shoulders with other people but fundamentally alone.

Humans are by far the most empathic species on the planet. Our remarkable capabilities rely on three neural systems that simulate another person's actions, emotions, and thoughts.

Actions

Networks in your brain's perceptual-motor systems light up both when you perform an action and when you see someone else perform that action, giving you a felt sense of what he's experiencing in his body (Oberman and Ramachandran 2007). In effect, these networks mirror the behavior of others, thus the common term, *mirror neurons.*

Emotions

The insula and linked circuits activate when you experience strong emotions such as fear or anger; they also light up when you see others having those same feelings, particularly people you care about. The more aware you are of your own emotional and bodily states, the more your insula and anterior cingulate cortex activate—and the better you are at reading others (Singer et al. 2004). In effect, the limbic networks that produce your feelings also make sense of the feelings of others. As a result, impairments in the expression of emotions—such as from a stroke—frequently also worsen the recognition of emotions in other people (Niedenthal 2007).

Thoughts

Psychologists use the term *theory of mind* (ToM), to refer to your ability to think about the inner workings of another person. ToM relies on prefrontal and temporal lobe structures that are evolutionarily quite recent (Gallagher and Frith 2003). ToM capabilities first appear during the third and fourth years of life and don't develop fully until the complete *myelination*—the insulation of axons which speeds neural signals along—of the prefrontal cortex in the late teens or early twenties (Singer 2006).

These three systems—tracking the actions, emotions, and thoughts of other people—help each other. For example, sensorimotor and limbic resonance with the actions and emotions of others gives you lots of data for ToM-type processing. Then, once you form an educated guess—often within just a few seconds—you can test it out on your body and your feelings. Working together, these systems help you understand, from the inside out, what it is like to be another person. In the next chapter, we'll cover a variety of ways to strengthen them.

LOVE AND ATTACHMENT

As the human brain evolved and grew larger, childhood grew longer (Coward 2008). Consequently, hominid bands had to evolve ways to keep their members connected for many years in order to sustain—in the African proverb—"the village it takes to raise a child" and thus pass on the band's genes (Gibbons 2008). To accomplish this, the brain acquired powerful circuitry and neurochemistry to generate and maintain love and attachment.

This is the physical foundation on which your mind has built your experiences of romance, heartache, and deep affection, and your bonds with family members. Of course, there is much more to love than the brain: culture, gender, and personal psychology play major roles as well. Nonetheless, a lot of research in developmental neuropsychology has shed light on why love can go so wrong—and how to set it right.

Love Feels Good

Romantic love is found in almost all human cultures, suggesting that it's deep in our biological—even our biochemical—nature (Jankowiak and Fischer 1992). Although endorphins and vasopressin are involved in the neurochemistry of bonding and love, the major player is probably oxytocin (Young and Wang 2004). This neuromodulator (and hormone) creates feelings of caring and cherishing; it's present in both females and males, though much more so in women. Oxytocin encourages eye-to-eye contact (Guastella, Mitchell, and Dads 2008); increases trust (Kosfeld et al. 2005); dampens amygdala arousal and promotes approach-type behaviors

(Petrovic et al. 2008); and supports tend-and-befriend behaviors in women when they're stressed (Taylor et al. 2000).

Distinct neural networks handle infatuation and long-term attachment (Fisher, Aron, and Brown 2006). In its early stages, it's natural for a romantic relationship to be dominated by intense, often volatile rewards that draw heavily on dopamine-based neural networks (Aron et al. 2005). Later, the relationship shifts gradually toward more diffuse and stable fulfillments that rely on oxytocin and related systems. Still, in long-term couples who continue to feel deeply in love, ongoing tickles of dopamine keep stimulating the pleasure centers of each partner's brain (Schechner 2008).

Losing Love Feels Bad

Besides pursuing the pleasure of love, we try to avoid the pain of it ending. When lovers get jilted, part of their limbic system lights up—the same part that activates when making high-risk investments that could end really badly (Fisher, Aron, and Brown 2006). Physical pain and social pain are based on overlapping neural systems (Eisenberger and Lieberman 2004): quite literally, rejection hurts.

Children and Attachment

When combined with other influences—e.g., psychological, cultural, and situational—these neurobiological factors often lead, no surprise, to babies. Here, too, oxytocin promotes bonding, particularly in the mother.

Children evolved to be lovable and parents to be loving, since strong attachments promote survival in the wild. The attachment system draws on multiple neural networks—which handle empathy, self-awareness, attention, emotion regulation, and motivation—to weave strong connections between a child and her parents (Siegel 2001). The recurring experiences a young child has with her caregivers course through these neural networks, molding them and thus the way the child relates to others and feels about herself. Hopefully all goes well—but these experiences occur at an age when children are most vulnerable, and their parents are usually most stressed and depleted (Hanson, Hanson, and Pollycove 2002), which creates inherent challenges. The human parent-child relationship is unique in the animal kingdom, and it has a singular power to shape how each of us pursues and expresses love as an adult; in the next chapter we'll explore how to work with the ways you may have been affected yourself.

THE WOLF OF HATE

Our unique evolutionary background has made us wonderfully cooperative, empathic, and loving. So why is our history so full of selfishness, cruelty, and violence?

Economic and cultural factors certainly play a role. Nonetheless, across different kinds of societies—hunter-gatherer, agrarian, and industrial; communist and capitalist; Eastern and Western—in most cases the story is basically the same: loyalty and protection toward "us," and fear and aggression toward "them." We've already seen how that stance toward "us" is deep in our nature. Now let's investigate how fear and aggression developed toward "them."

Nasty and Brutish

For millions of years, our ancestors were exposed to starvation, predators, and disease. Making matters worse, climactic ups and downs brought scorching droughts and freezing ice ages, intensifying the competition for scarce resources. Altogether, these harsh conditions kept hominid and human population levels essentially flat despite potential growth rates of about 2 percent per year (Bowles 2006).

In those tough environments, it was reproductively advantageous for our ancestors to be cooperative within their own band but aggressive toward other bands (Choi and Bowles 2007). Cooperation and aggression evolved synergistically: bands with greater cooperation were more successful at aggression, and aggression between bands demanded cooperation within bands (Bowles 2009).

Much like cooperation and love draw on multiple neurological systems, so do aggression and hate:

- Much if not most aggression is a response to feeling threatened—which includes even subtle feelings of unease or anxiety. Because the amygdala is *primed* to register threats and is increasingly sensitized by what it "perceives," many people feel increasingly threatened over time. And thus increasingly aggressive.

- Once the SNS/HPAA system activates, if you're going to fight instead of flee, blood surges to your arm muscles for hitting, *piloerection* (goose bumps) makes your hair stand up to make you look more intimidating to a potential attacker or predator, and the hypothalamus can—in the extreme—trigger rage reactions.

- Aggressiveness correlates with high testosterone—in both men and women—and low serotonin.

- Language systems in the left frontal and temporal lobes work with visual-spatial processing in the right hemisphere to categorize others as friends or foes, persons or nonentities.

- "Hot" aggression—with lots of SNS/HPAA activation—often overwhelms prefrontal regulation of emotions. "Cold" aggression involves little SNS/HPAA activation and draws on sustained prefrontal activity; consider the proverb "revenge is a dish best served cold."

The result of these neural dynamics is a familiar one: take good care of "us," and fear, disdain, and attack "them." For example, research suggests that most modern hunter-gatherer bands—which offer strong indications of the social environments in which our ancestors evolved—have engaged in ongoing conflicts with other groups. While these skirmishes lacked the shock and awe of modern warfare, they were actually much more lethal: roughly one in eight hunter-gatherer males died from them, compared to the one in a hundred men who died from the wars of the twentieth century (Bowles 2006; Keeley 1997).

Our brains still possess these capabilities and inclinations. They're at work in schoolyard cliques, office politics, and domestic violence. (Healthy competition, assertiveness, and fierce advocacy for people and causes you care about are very different from hostile aggression.) On a larger scale, our aggressive tendencies fuel prejudice, oppression, ethnic cleansing, and war. Often these tendencies are manipulated, such as by the demonization of "them" in the classic justification for strong-father, authoritarian control. But those manipulations wouldn't be nearly so successful if it weren't for the legacy of between-group aggression in our evolutionary history.

What's Left Out?

The wolf of love sees a vast horizon, with all beings included in the circle of "us." That circle shrinks down for the wolf of hate, so that only the nation, or tribe, or friends and family—or, in the extreme, only the individual self—is held as "us," surrounded by threatening masses of "them." In fact, sometimes the circle gets so small that one part of the mind is hateful toward another part. For example, I've had clients who could not look in the mirror because they thought they were so ugly.

There's a Zen saying, *Nothing left out.* Nothing left out of your awareness, nothing left out of your practice, nothing left out of your heart. As the circle shrinks, the question naturally arises: What is left out? It could be people on the other side of the world with a different religion, or people next door whose politics you don't like. Or relatives who are difficult, or old friends who hurt you. It could be anyone you regard as less than you or as merely a means to your ends.

As soon as you place anyone outside of the circle of "us," the mind/brain automatically begins to devalue that person and justify poor treatment of him (Efferson, Lalive, and Feh 2008). This gets the wolf of hate up and moving, only a quick pounce away from active aggression. Pay attention to the number of times a day you categorize someone as "not like me," particularly in subtle ways: not my social background, not my style, and so on. It's startling how routine it is. See what happens to your mind when you consciously release this distinction and focus instead on what you have in common with that person, on what makes you both an "us."

Ironically, one answer to "What's left out?" is the wolf of hate itself, which is often denied or minimized. For example, it makes me uncomfortable to admit how good it feels when the hero kills the bad guy in a movie. Like it or not, the wolf of hate is alive and well inside each one of us. It's easy to hear about a dreadful murder across the country or terrorism and torture across the world—or milder forms of everyday mistreatment of others close at hand— and shake your head, thinking, "What's wrong with them?" But them is actually *us*. We all have the same basic DNA. It is a kind of ignorance—which is the root of suffering—to deny the aggression in our genetic endowment. In fact, as we've seen, intense intergroup conflict aided the evolution of within-group altruism: the wolf of hate helped give birth to the wolf of love.

The wolf of hate is deeply embedded both in the human evolutionary past and in each person's brain today, ready to howl at any threat. Being realistic and honest about the wolf of hate—and its impersonal, evolutionary origins—brings self-compassion. Your own wolf of hate needs taming, sure, but it's not your fault that it lurks in the shadows of your mind, and it probably afflicts you more than anyone else. Additionally, acknowledging the wolf of hate prompts a very useful caution when you are in situations— arguing with a neighbor, disciplining a child, reacting to criticism at work—in which you feel mistreated and revved-up, and that wolf begins to stir.

When you're watching the evening news—or even just listening to children bicker—it can sometimes seem like the wolf of hate dominates human existence. Much like spikes of SNS/HPAA arousal stand out against a backdrop of resting-state parasympathetic activation, dark clouds of aggression and conflict compel more attention than the much larger "sky" of connection and love through which they pass. But in fact, most interactions have a cooperative quality. Humans and other primate species routinely restrain the wolf of hate and repair its damage, returning to a baseline of reasonably positive relationships with each other (Sapolsky 2006). In most people most of the time, the wolf of love is bigger and stronger than the wolf of hate.

Love and hate: they live and tumble together in every heart, like wolf cubs tussling in a cave. There is no killing the wolf of hate; the aversion in such an attempt would actually create what you're trying to destroy. But you can watch that wolf carefully, keep it tethered, and limit its alarm, righteousness, grievances, resentments, contempt, and prejudice. Meanwhile, keep nourishing and encouraging the wolf of love. We'll explore how to do that in the next two chapters.

---

chapter 8: KEY POINTS

🏵 Each of us has two wolves in the heart, one of love and one of hate. Everything depends on which one we feed each day.

🏵 While the wolf of hate gets more press, the wolf of love is actually bigger and stronger, and its development over millions of years has been a major factor in driving the evolution of the brain. For example, mammals and birds have bigger brains than reptiles and fish in large part to manage relationships with mates and offspring. And the more sociable the primate species, the bigger the brain.

☙ The size of the human brain has tripled in the past three million years; much of this growth is devoted to interpersonal capabilities such as empathy and cooperative planning. In the harsh conditions faced by our ancestors, cooperation aided survival; thus, factors that promote cooperation have been woven into your brain. These include altruism, generosity, concern about reputation, fairness, language, forgiveness, and morality and religion.

☙ Empathy relies on three neural systems that simulate the actions, emotions, and thoughts of others.

☙ As the brain grew in size, early humans needed a longer childhood to develop and train the brain; and as childhood grew longer, our ancestors needed to find new ways to bond parents and children and other members of the band in order to preserve "the village it takes to raise a child." Multiple neural networks accomplish this, such as reward systems based on dopamine and oxytocin and punishment systems in which social rejection creates activation much like physical pain does.

☙ Meanwhile, the wolf of hate also evolved. Hunter-gatherer bands frequently engaged in highly lethal violence toward each other. Within-group cooperation made between-group aggression more successful, and the rewards of that aggression—food, mates, survival—promoted within-group cooperation. Cooperation and aggression—love and hate—co-evolved synergistically. Their capabilities and inclinations remain within us today.

☙ The wolf of hate shrinks the circle of "us," sometimes to the point that only the self is left inside it. The brain routinely categorizes "us" and "them," and then automatically prefers "us" and devalues "them."

🪷 Ironically, sometimes the wolf of hate is set outside the circle of "us." But there is no killing the wolf of hate, and denying it just lets it grow in the shadows. We need to acknowledge the wolf of hate and appreciate the power of the wolf of love—and then restrain the one while feeding the other.

chapter 9

Compassion and Assertion

If we could read the secret history of our enemies,
we should find in each [person's] life sorrow
and suffering enough to disarm any hostility.

—Henry Wadsworth Longfellow

I sat on the board of a meditation center for nine years, and was often struck by how its teachers expressed their views. They were compassionate about the concerns of others, but when they said what they thought, they did so clearly and often strongly, without hemming or hawing. And then they let it be, not becoming defensive or argumentative. This combination of openheartedness and directness was very powerful. It got the job done while nurturing the love in the room.

This was compassion and assertion working together. They're the two wings that get any relationship off the ground and keep it flying. They support each other: compassion brings caring to assertion, while assertion helps you feel comfortable giving compassion since you know your own needs will be met. Compassion widens the circle of "us" while assertion protects and supports everyone inside it. They both nourish the wolf of love. In this chapter, we'll explore brain-savvy ways to use and strengthen your inborn abilities to be compassionate and assertive, and we'll begin with compassion.

In order to be truly compassionate, you must first feel something of what the other person is going through. You must have empathy, which cuts through the automatic tendencies of the brain that create an "us" and a "them." So that's where we'll start.

EMPATHY

Empathy is the foundation of any meaningful relationship. When someone empathizes with you, it gives you the sense that your inner being truly exists for that person—that you are a Thou to his I, with feelings and needs that have standing. Empathy reassures you that he understands your inner workings at least somewhat, particularly your intentions and emotions. We are social animals, who, as Dan Siegel puts it, need to feel *felt* (2007).

Or let's say you are the one who is offering empathy. Empathy is respectful and soothing, and it usually evokes goodwill in return. Often empathy is all the other person is asking of you; if there is still something the person needs to talk about, you can address it in a more positive atmosphere. Further, being empathic gives you lots of useful information about the other person, including what's really on her mind, and what she really cares about. For example, if she's being critical of you, sense down into her deeper wants, particularly the softer and younger ones. Then you'll have a fuller picture, which will probably reduce any frustration or anger toward her. She'll likely sense this shift in you, and become more understanding herself.

To be clear: empathy is neither agreement nor approval. You can empathize with someone you wish would act differently. Empathy *doesn't* mean waiving your rights; knowing this can help you feel it's alright to be empathic.

In spiritual practice, empathy sees how we are all related to each other. It is mindful and curious, with a "don't know" quality that prevents you from getting stuck in your own views. Empathy is virtue in action, the restraint of reactive patterns in order to stay present with another person. It embodies non-harming, since a lack of empathy is often upsetting to others, and also opens the door to hurting them unwittingly. Empathy contains an inherent generosity: you give the willingness to be moved by another person.

Empathic Breakdowns

For all its benefits, empathy disappears quickly during most conflicts, and fades away slowly in many long-term relationships. Unfortunately, inadequate empathy erodes trust and makes it harder to solve interpersonal problems. Just recall a time you felt misunderstood—or worse, a time when the other person didn't even want to understand you. A history of empathic breakdowns has effects; the more vulnerable a person is and the higher the stakes, the greater the impact. For example, insufficient caregiver empathy often leads to insecure attachment in a young child. In the larger world, empathic breakdowns lead to exploitation, prejudice, and terrible atrocities. There's no empathy in the wolf of hate.

How to Be Empathic

Your natural capacity for empathy can be brought forth deliberately, used skillfully, and strengthened. Here's how to work with the brain's empathy circuits.

SET THE STAGE

Bring conscious intention to being empathic. For example, when I realize that my wife wants to have one of *those* conversations—

she's not happy about something, and it's probably me—I try to take a few seconds to remind myself to be empathic and not lame, and that it feels good to be empathic. These little steps activate the prefrontal cortex (PFC) to orient you to the situation, focus your intentions, and prime empathy-related neural networks; they also warm up the limbic system to get your brain headed toward the rewards of empathy.

Next, relax your body and mind, and open to the other person as much as feels right to you. Use the methods in the next section to feel safe and strong enough to receive the other person fully. Remind yourself that whatever is in his mind is over *there*, and you're over *here*, present with but separate from the stream of his thoughts and feelings.

Keep paying attention to the other person; be *with* him. This sort of sustained attention is uncommon, and other people appreciate it a lot. Appoint a little guardian in your mind that keeps watching the continuity of your attentiveness; this will stimulate the anterior cingulate cortex (ACC), which pays attention to attention. (We'll say more about this guardian in chapter 12.) In a way, empathy is a kind of mindfulness meditation focused on someone else's inner world.

NOTICE THE ACTIONS OF OTHERS

Notice the other person's movements, stance, gestures, and actions. (The point is to energize the perceptual-motor mirroring functions of your brain, not to analyze her body language.) Imagine doing these yourself. What would it feel like, in your own body, to do them? If it's appropriate, match some of her movements unobtrusively with your own, and notice what this feels like.

SENSE THE FEELINGS OF OTHERS

Tune in to yourself. Sense your breathing, body, and emotions. As we've seen, this stimulates your insula and primes it to sense the inner feelings of others.

Watch the other person's face and eyes closely. Our core emotions are expressed through universal facial expressions (Ekman 2007). They often flit by quickly, but if you're mindful, you can spot them. This is the biological basis for the old saying that the eyes are the windows to the soul.

Relax. Let your body open to resonating with the other person's emotions.

TRACK THE THOUGHTS OF OTHERS

Actively imagine what the other person could be thinking and wanting. Imagine what could be going on beneath the surface, and what might be pulling in different directions inside him. Consider what you know or can reasonably guess about him, such as his personal history, childhood, temperament, personality, "hot buttons," recent events in his life, and the nature of his relationship with you: What effect might these have? Also take into account what you've already experienced from tuning in to his actions and emotions. Ask yourself questions, such as *What might he be feeling deep down? What could be most important to him? What might he want from me?* Be respectful, and don't jump to conclusions: stay in "don't know" mind.

CHECK BACK

As appropriate, check with the other person to see if you're on the right track. For example, you might say, "Sounds like you're feeling _____, is that right?" Or, "I'm not sure, but I get the sense that _____." Or, "It seems like what bothered you was _____. Did you want _____?"

Be careful not to ask questions in an argumentative or prosecutorial way to advance your own viewpoint. And don't muddle empathy together with any disagreements you may have. Keep empathy separate from asserting yourself, and try to be clear about the transition from one to the other. For example, you might say something like,

"I get that you wanted more attention from me when we visited my relatives, and that you felt bad. It makes sense to me and I'm sorry. I'm going to be more careful about that in the future. [Pause.] But, you know, you seemed happy chatting away with Aunt Sue and didn't tell me that you wanted more attention. If you could tell me directly what you'd like in the moment, it would be easier for me to give it to you—which is what I definitely want to do."

RECEIVE EMPATHY YOURSELF

When you would like to receive empathy, remember that you're more likely to get it if you are "feelable." Be open, present, and honest. You could also ask for empathy directly; remember that some people may just not realize that receiving empathy is important to you (and to lots of others, too). Be willing to say explicitly what you would like to receive. It often helps to make it clear that it's empathy you want, not necessarily agreement or approval. When you sense that the other person gets how it is for you, at least in some ways, let the experience of receiving empathy sink into your implicit, emotional memory.

FEELING COMFORTABLE WITH CLOSENESS

Empathy opens you up to other people and naturally draws you closer. So to be as empathic as possible, you need to be comfortable with closeness. But this can be challenging. During our evolutionary history, there were many risks in encounters with others. Additionally, most psychological pain occurs in close relationships—particularly those in early childhood, when memory networks are most easily shaped and emotional reactions are least regulated by the PFC. All in all, it's natural to be wary about getting too close. The methods below can help you feel safer while becoming more deeply connected with other people.

Focus on Your Internal Experience

There appears to be a central network in the middle and lower regions of the brain that evolved to integrate multiple social-emotional capabilities (Siegel 2007). This network is stimulated by important relationships, especially their emotional aspects. Depending somewhat on your temperament (some of us are more affected by relationships than others), you might feel flooded by all the information flowing through this network. To deal with this, focus more on your own experience than on the other person (e.g., track some breaths in and out, or wiggle your toes and pay attention to the sensations). Notice how you keep going on being, doing just fine even though you are emotionally close. This reduces the sense of threat from closeness and thus the desire to pull back.

Pay Attention to Awareness Itself

Pay attention to awareness itself, distinct from the (potentially intense) sense of the other person contained within awareness; simply notice that you're aware and explore what that's like. Technically, the working memory aspects of awareness appear to be based largely on neural substrates in the *dorsolateral* (upper-outer) portions of the PFC, in contrast to the *ventromedial* (lower-middle) circuitry that processes social-emotional content. By bringing attention to awareness, you're probably energizing those dorsolateral circuits more than their ventromedial neighbors.

Use Imagery

Use imagery, which stimulates the right hemisphere of your brain. For example, if I'm with someone who's getting intense, I might imagine myself as a deeply rooted tree, with the other person's attitudes and emotions blowing through my leaves and shaking them—but winds always come to an end, and my tree remains standing. Or I'll imagine that there is a picket fence between us—or, if need be, a glass wall that's a foot thick. In addition to the benefits that come from the particular images themselves, activating the right hemisphere encourages a sense of the whole that is larger than any part—including that part of your experience which might feel uncomfortable with closeness.

Be Mindful of Your Inner World

Whether you're with others or by yourself, being mindful of your inner world seems to help heal significant shortages of empathy you may have experienced when you were young (Siegel 2007). In essence, mindful attention to your own experience activates many of the same circuits that are stimulated in childhood by the attuned and caring attention of others. Thus, you're giving to yourself here and now what you should have gotten when you were little; over time, this interest and concern will gradually sink in, helping you feel more secure while being close with others.

MAY YOU NOT SUFFER

You can deliberately cultivate compassion, which will stimulate and strengthen its underlying neural substrate, including your ACC and insula (Lutz, Brefczynski-Lewis, et al. 2008). To prime the neural circuits of compassion, bring to mind the feeling of being with someone who loves you, while calling up heartfelt emotions such as gratitude or fondness. Next, bring empathy to the difficulties of the other person. Opening to his (even subtle) suffering, let sympathy and goodwill naturally arise. (These steps flow together in actual practice.)

Then, in your mind, offer explicit wishes, such as *May you not suffer. May you find rest. May it go well with the doctor.* Or wordlessly experience compassionate feelings and wishes. You could also focus on universal, nonreferential compassion—compassion which has no particular target—so that, as Tibetan monk Mathieu Ricard says, "benevolence and compassion pervade the mind as a way of being" (Lutz, Brefczynski-Lewis, et al. 2008, e1897).

You can also bring compassion practices into meditation. In the beginning, make your compassionate phrases the object of attention. As the meditation deepens, sink into feeling compassion beyond words, the sense of it filling your heart and chest and body, becoming increasingly absorbing and intense. You may feel compassion radiating from you in all directions: front and back, left and right, up and down.

However and whenever you experience compassion, be mindful of the experience and really take it in. By remembering what it's like, you'll be more able to return to this lovely state of mind in the future.

Every day, try to have compassion for five kinds of people: someone you're grateful to (a "benefactor"), a loved one or friend, a neutral person, someone who is difficult for you—and yourself. For example, sometimes I'll look at a stranger on the street (a neutral person), get a quick sense of him or her, and then access a sense of compassion. You can also bring compassion to animals and plants, or toward groups of people (e.g., children, those who are ill, Republicans or Democrats). Compassion is for *everyone*.

Even though it can be hard to bring compassion to a difficult person, doing so reinforces the important lesson that we are all one in our suffering. When you see how connected everything is, and the many factors "upstream" that push on every person, compassion naturally arises. The Buddhist image of this is the jewel of compassion resting in the lotus of wisdom—the union of caring and insight.

ASSERTING YOURSELF

Being assertive means speaking your truth and pursuing your aims in the nitty-gritty of relationships. In my experience, skillful assertiveness is founded on *unilateral virtue* and *effective communica-*

tion. Let's see what this actually means, whether interacting with a friend, coworker, lover, or family member.

Unilateral Virtue

Virtue sounds lofty, but it's actually down to earth. It simply means living from your innate goodness, guided by principle. When you are virtuous no matter what other people do, their behavior is not controlling you. As a therapist, I've seen many couples in which each person says essentially the same thing: *I'll treat you well after you treat me well.* They're stuck in a standoff—which neither one of them truly wants—because they're each letting the other person determine their behavior.

On the other hand, when you are unilaterally virtuous, you head directly toward your own enlightened self-interest whether or not the other person cooperates. It feels good to be good, enjoying "the bliss of blamelessness" with a mind untroubled by guilt or regret. Staying principled fosters inner peace by reducing wrangles that would otherwise weigh on your mind. It increases the odds that others will treat you well in return. If need be, it sets you on the moral high ground.

To attain this quality of deep insight, we must have a mind that is quiet and malleable. Achieving such a state of mind requires that we first develop the ability to regulate our body and speech so as to cause no conflict.
—Venerable Tenzin Palmo

Doing the right thing draws on both head and heart. Your prefrontal cortex ("head") forms values, makes plans, and gives instructions to the rest of the brain. Your limbic system ("heart") fuels the inner strength you use to do the right thing when it's hard, and supports heart-centered virtues such as courage, generosity, and forgiveness. Even seemingly "heady" moral reasoning draws heavily on emotional processing; consequently, people with damage to the limbic system have a hard time making certain ethical decisions (Haidt 2007).

Virtue in the mind is supported by regulation in the brain. Both of these involve finding an equilibrium that is centered around healthy core aims, stays in bounds, and changes smoothly rather than abruptly or chaotically. To find that place of balance for yourself, let's apply the nature of a healthy equilibrium to virtue. Then you'll develop your own "code." Throughout this exploration, keep listening to both your head and your heart for what it would mean to assert yourself virtuously.

AN EQUILIBRIUM OF VIRTUE

First, identify your core aims. What are your purposes and principles in relationships? For example, one fundamental moral value is not to harm people, including yourself. If your needs are not being met in a relationship, that's harmful to you. If you are mean or punishing, that harms others. Another potential aim might be to keep discovering the truth about yourself and the other person.

Second, stay in bounds. The Wise Speech section of Buddhism's Noble Eightfold Path offers good guidelines for communication that stays within the lines: *Say only what is well-intended, true, beneficial, timely, expressed without harshness or malice, and—ideally— what is wanted.* Several years ago I took up the precept of never speaking or acting out of anger. I must have violated it that first day in a dozen little ways, with exasperation, sarcasm, eye rolls, sniffs, whatever. But over time it's become more ingrained, and a very powerful practice. It forces a person to slow down in interactions, to avoid making matters worse by pouring the gasoline of anger on a smoldering fire, and to feel down below for the real issue (e.g., hurt, worry, guilt). Afterward, you feel good about yourself: you stayed in control and didn't add your own reactivity to a tense situation. Of course, the principle of staying in bounds applies to others, too. If someone violates your boundaries—for example, by treating you disrespectfully, or continuing to yell at you after you say you want it to stop—that pushes the equilibrium of your relationship out of bounds, and your code can certainly include not putting up with that. (We'll explore how to stand up for yourself in the section below on effective communication.)

Third, change smoothly. In a series of studies (1995), psychologist John Gottman documented the value of a slow start-up when discussing potentially upsetting matters with another person. As I've learned myself, that usually works a lot better than doing things like walking in the front door and immediately criticizing your partner for having all the lights on. Rapid, abrupt actions trigger alarms in the other person's SNS/HPAA system, which shake a relationship like poking a sleeping cat with a sharp stick. Small but skillful steps prevent these herky-jerky shifts—steps, such as asking if this is a good time to talk before diving in full steam, or not curtly cutting off a conversation that's striking too close to home.

PERSONAL CODE

Now write your personal code of unilateral relationship virtues. This could be a handful of words. Or more extensive dos and don'ts. Whatever its form, aim for language that is powerful and motivating, that makes sense to your head and touches your heart. It doesn't have to be perfect to be useful, and you can always revise it later. For example, it might include statements like these:

Listen more, talk less.

Don't yell or threaten other people, and don't let them do that to me.

Every day, ask my wife three questions in a row about how things are going for her.

Get home by six every night to have dinner with the family.

Say what I need.

Be loving.

Keep my promises.

When you're done, visualize yourself acting according to your code no matter what happens. Imagine the good feelings and other rewards that this will bring you. Take these in to help motivate yourself to truly live by your code. Then, when you do live by it and things go well, take that in, too.

EFFECTIVE COMMUNICATION

Lots can be said about how to communicate effectively. From thirty-plus years of working with people as a therapist or management consultant—and some painful lessons as a husband and father—I consider these the key points:

- Stay in touch with your deeper feelings and wants. The mind is like a giant parfait, with softer, child-like, and more essential layers under harder, adult-like, and more superficial ones. Based on this inner mindfulness, keep clarifying your aims in the interaction. For example, do you just want to be listened to? Is there something in particular you want to be sure will never happen again?

- Take responsibility for getting your needs met in the relationship. Stay focused on the prize, whatever it is for you, and keep coming back to it. If the other person has important topics of his own, often it works best to take turns, focusing on one topic at a time, rather than mixing them together.

- Communicate primarily for yourself, not to produce a particular response from the other person. Sure, it's reasonable to hope for some good results over there. But if you communicate in order to fix, change, or convince another person, the success of your communications will depend on how she reacts to you, and then it's out of your hands. Plus, the other person is likely to be more open to you if she doesn't feel pressed to change in some way.

- Stay guided by your personal code. At the end of the day, what you and the other person will mainly remember is not what you said but *how* you said it. Be careful about your tone, and avoid language that is fault-finding, exaggerated, or inflammatory.

- When you speak, keep coming back to your own experience—notably, your emotions, body sensations, and underlying hopes and wishes—rather than talking about events, such as the other person's actions, and your opinions about them. No one can argue with your experience; it is what it is, and you are the world's expert on it. When you share your experience, take responsibility for it, and don't blame the other person for it. As appropriate, convey its deeper layers, such as the longings for love that lie beneath jealousy. Even though this openness is often scary, the deeper layers contain what's most vital to get at for both you and the other person. The universality of these layers and their relatively unthreatening nature also increase the chance that the other person will lower his guard and hear what you have to say. I highly recommend the approach Marshall Rosenberg details in *Nonviolent Communication* (2nd Edition 2008), which has essentially three parts: *When X happens* [described factually, not judgmentally], *I feel Y* [especially the deeper, softer emotions], *because I need Z* [fundamental needs and wants].

- Try to experience your truth as you speak it. This will increase your inner mindfulness, and probably also help the other person empathize with you. Notice any tightness in the eyes, throat, chest, belly, or floor of the pelvis, and see if you can relax it to allow your experience to flow more freely.

- Use the power of embodied emotion: take the physical stance of a feeling or attitude—which might not be your usual posture—to aid the expression of it (Niedenthal 2007). For example, if you typically hold back, try talking while leaning slightly forward; if you tend to push away sadness, soften your eyes; if you find it hard to be assertive, shift your shoulders to open your chest.

- If you think you might get triggered by the interaction and lose your way, help your prefrontal cortex to help you—an interesting circularity!—by sorting out your key points in advance, even writing them down. To keep your words and tone clean, imagine a video recording being made of your interaction: act so that you wouldn't wince if you saw it.

- If you are solving a problem with someone, establish the facts (if you can). This usually narrows the disagreement and brings in useful information. But mainly focus on the future, not the past. Most quarrels are about the past: what happened, how bad it was, who said what, how it was said, extenuating circumstances, and so on. Instead, try to agree about how things will be *from now on*. Be as clear as possible. If it helps, write it down. Tacitly or explicitly, you are making agreements with each other that should be taken as seriously as commitments at work.

- Take maximum reasonable responsibility for the other person's issues with you. Identify what there is to correct on your part, and correct it unilaterally—even if that person keeps blowing it with you. One by one, keep crossing off her legitimate complaints. It's fine to put some attention on trying to influence her behavior, but focus mainly on being honorable, benevolent, and increasingly skillful yourself. This is definitely the road less traveled, but it's the one that's both kind and smart. You can't control how she treats you, but you *can* control how you treat her: these are the causes you can actually tend to. And doing what's right regardless of her behavior is a good way to encourage her to treat you well.

- Give it time. As time passes—weeks and months, not years—the truth about the other person will become clearer. For example: Does he respect your boundaries? Will he keep agreements? Can he repair misunderstandings? What is his learning curve for self-understanding and interpersonal skills (appropriate to the type of relationship)? What are his true intentions (revealed over time by his actions)?

- When you see another person clearly, sometimes you realize that the relationship needs to change to match what you can actually count on. This goes two ways: a relationship that's bigger than its real foundation is a set-up for disappointment and hurt, while a relationship that's smaller than its foundation is a lost opportunity. In both cases, focus on your own initiative, especially after you've made reasonable efforts to encourage changes in the other person.

  For example, you usually can't make a coworker stop being dismissive of you, but you can "shrink" the relationship—so it's closer to the size of its true foundation—by minimizing your contacts with him, doing an excellent job on your own, building up alliances with other people, and arranging for the quality of your work to be seen widely. Conversely, if there is a large foundation of love in your marriage but your mate is not that emotionally nurturing, you can try to "grow" the relationship on your own by paying particular attention to when he expresses caring through his actions and soaking that into your heart, by drawing him into situations with a culture of warmth (e.g., dinner with friends, certain kinds of live music, meditation group), and perhaps by being more emotionally nurturing yourself.

- Throughout all of this, keep in mind the big picture, the 1,000-foot view. See the impermanence of whatever is at issue, and the many causes and conditions that led to it. See the collateral damage—the suffering—that results when you cling to your desires and opinions or take things personally. Over the long haul, most of what we argue about with others really doesn't matter that much.

- Above all, try to preserve your fundamental orientation of compassion and kindness. You can differ vigorously with people while simultaneously holding them in your heart. For example, bearing in mind all that has happened in Tibet since it was invaded in 1950, consider how the Dalai Lama has spoken of the Chinese government as: *my friend, the enemy* (Brehony 2001, 217). Or consider Nelson Mandela, imprisoned for twenty-seven years—much of that time doing hard labor in a quarry—often receiving mail just once every six months. It's said that he despaired of losing contact with people he loved, so he decided to bring love to his guards while continuing to stand firm in his opposition to apartheid. It was hard for the guards to mistreat him when he was being loving, so the authorities had to keep replacing them, but Mandela would just love the new ones, too. In fact, at his inauguration as president of South Africa, one of his former guards was seated in the front row.

chapter 9: KEY POINTS

◉ Compassion is concern for the suffering of beings (including yourself). Assertion is expressing your truth and pursuing your aims within any type of relationship. These two work together. Compassion infuses warmth and caring into your assertiveness. Assertiveness helps you stick up for yourself and others, and to feel confident that you can still get your needs met even while being compassionate.

◉ Empathy is the basis of true compassion, since it makes you aware of the difficulties others face and their suffering. Empathy supports relationships in other ways as well, such as by helping you understand another person's inner workings. Empathic breakdowns are upsetting. When they happen frequently with vulnerable people such as children, they can be very harmful.

◉ Empathy involves simulating the actions, feelings, and thoughts of another person. Simulate her actions through imagining what it would feel like in your body to do them. Simulate her feelings through tuning into your own emotions and watching her face and eyes closely. Simulate her thoughts by taking into account what you know about her, and by forming good guesses about her inner world.

◉ Being comfortable with closeness supports empathy and compassion. Nonetheless, humanity's evolutionary heritage (in which the greatest threats usually came from other people), combined with personal life experiences (especially childhood ones), can make an individual uncomfortable with closeness. Ways to increase comfort with closeness include focusing on your internal experience instead of on the other person, paying attention to awareness itself, using imagery, and being mindful of your inner world.

♨ Compassion draws on the anterior cingulate cortex (ACC) and insula. Through cultivating compassion, you can strengthen the circuitry in these regions.

♨ Compassion is supported by recalling the feeling of being with someone who loves you, evoking heartfelt emotions such as gratitude, being empathic, opening to the suffering of other beings, and wishing them well. Bring compassion to five kinds of people: benefactors, friends, neutral people, difficult people, and yourself.

♨ Asserting yourself skillfully involves unilateral virtue and effective communication. Virtue means living from your innate goodness, guided by principle. Virtue in your mind rests on regulation in your brain; both virtue and regulation require maintaining a balance that is centered around healthy aims, stays within a healthy range, and changes smoothly.

♨ After considering your aims in relationships, what it means to stay in bounds, and how to interact harmoniously with others, establish your personal code of relationship virtues. Living by this code unilaterally—no matter what others do—increases your independence and self-control in relationships, feels good in its own right, puts you on the moral high ground, and is your best-odds strategy for evoking good behavior from others.

♨ Key points for effective communication include: focus on speaking your truth rather than changing other people; stay in touch with your experience, especially the deeper layers; establish the facts; take maximum reasonable responsibility for the other person's issues with you and keep addressing his or her legitimate complaints; do what you can to have the relationship match its true foundation; keep in mind the big picture; and maintain compassion and kindness.

chapter 10

Boundless Kindness

All joy in this world comes from wanting others
to be happy, and all suffering in this world comes
from wanting only oneself to be happy.

—Shantideva

I f compassion is the wish that beings not suffer, kindness is the wish that they be happy. Compassion responds primarily to suffering, but kindness comes into play all of the time, even when others are doing fine. Kindness is expressed mainly in small, everyday ways, such as leaving a big tip, reading one more story to a child even though you're tired, or waving another driver to move ahead of you in traffic.

Kindness has a loving quality, thus the term *loving-kindness.* Loving-kindness ranges from the casual helpfulness of strangers to the profound love one has for a child or mate. The words "kind" and "kin," share the same root; kindness brings people into the circle of "us" and feeds the wolf of love.

Kindness depends on prefrontal intentions and principles, limbic-based emotions and rewards, neurochemicals such as oxytocin and endorphins, and brain stem arousal. These factors offer you a variety of ways to nurture your kindness, which we'll explore in this chapter.

WISHING OTHERS WELL

I often work with children and have spent a lot of time in schools. I really like these guidelines I once saw posted in a kindergarten: *Be nice. Share your toys.* These are excellent intentions to be kind—and you don't need much more than them to steer your life!

Every morning, establish the intention to be kind and loving that day. Imagine the good feelings that will come from treating people with kindness; take in these feelings as rewards that will naturally draw your mind and brain toward kindness. The results could ripple far and wide.

One way to focus and express kind intentions is through these traditional wishes, which you can think, write down, or even sing:

May you be safe.

May you be healthy.

May you be happy.

May you live with ease.

You can modify these if you like, using whatever words evoke strong feelings of kindness and love in you. For example:

May you be safe from inner and outer harm.

May your body be strong and vital.

May you truly be at peace.

May you and everyone you love prosper.

May you be safe, healthy, happy, and at ease.

You can also be very specific:

May you get that job you want.

Susan, may your mother treat you well.

May you get a hit at Little League today, Carlo.

May I be at peace with my daughter.

Loving-kindness practice is like compassion practice in several ways. It involves both wishes and feelings; in your brain, loving-kindness mobilizes prefrontal language and intention networks as well as limbic emotion and reward networks. It calls on equanimity to keep the heart open, especially in the face of great pain or provocation. Kindness is for everyone—"omitting none," in the traditional phrase—with all beings held as "us" in your heart. There are five types of people you can offer kindness to: benefactors, friends, neutral people, difficult people, and yourself. When you are kind to someone else, you also benefit yourself; it feels good to be kind, and it encourages others to treat you well in turn.

You can even be kind to parts of yourself. For example, it's touching and powerful to be kind to the little child within you. You could also be kind to aspects of yourself that you wish were different, such as a craving for attention, a learning disability, or a fear of certain situations.

Loving-Kindness Meditation

You can meditate on loving-kindness itself; it has a warm feeling to it that is "juicier" than the breath and thus, for many people, easier to keep paying attention to. One practice is to express your kind wishes as specific phrases—such as the ones in the previous section—and then say them in your mind one by one, perhaps in rhythm with the breath (e.g., one phrase per breath). Or you can use the phrases more as a gentle guide, returning to them if your attention wanders. All the while, keep settling into the feeling of loving-kindness, in which there is boundless goodwill, generosity, and cherishing. You can use loving-kindness for deepening concentration: instead of becoming absorbed in the breath, you sink into loving-kindness. Meanwhile, loving-kindness is sinking into you; keep taking it into implicit memory, weaving its lovely threads into the fabric of your being.

When you try to offer loving-kindness to those in the category of "difficult people," it's natural to find this a challenge. First, establish some calm, stability, and spaciousness in your mind. Then work your way into it, starting with a person who is only mildly difficult for you, such as a coworker who's a little annoying but also has a lot of good qualities.

Kindness in Daily Life

Throughout the day, deliberately and actively bring kindness into your actions, your speech, and most of all, your thoughts. Try to encourage more themes of kindness in the mini-movies running in the background of your mind, in the simulator. As the simulator's neural networks increasingly "fire" with messages of kindness, that feeling and stance toward others will become more "wired" into your brain.

Try experiments in which you bring loving-kindness to someone for a specific period of time—perhaps a family member for an evening, or a coworker during a meeting—and see what happens. Also act kindly toward yourself—and see what that's like! My teacher, Jack Kornfield, sometimes encourages people to do a year of loving-kindness toward themselves, which is a powerful practice.

A Call to Love

Across all faiths and traditions, every great teacher has asked us to be loving and kind. Loving-kindness is not about being nice in some sentimental or superficial way: it is a fearless, passionate cherishing of everyone and everything, omitting none. Love is the jewel in the lotus, and it's just as important as wisdom. Love is a profound path of practice in its own right, as seen in the Buddha's reference to "the liberation of mind by loving-kindness."

TURNING ILL WILL TO GOODWILL

Kindness is relatively easy when others treat you well, or at least don't harm you. The acid test is to find your way to kindness even when you've been mistreated. The Jataka Tales describe the Buddha's (supposed) past lives as different animals, when animals could talk. For an example of unconditional loving-kindness, I've adapted a story in which he's a gorilla:

> One day a hunter came into the forest, got lost, fell down a deep hole, and couldn't climb out. He called for days, growing hungrier and weaker. Finally the Buddha-gorilla heard him and came. Seeing the steep and slippery sides of the hole, the gorilla told the man, "To carry you out safely, first I'm going to roll boulders down and practice on them."
>
> The gorilla rolled several boulders into the hole, each one bigger than the last, and carried them all out. Finally he was ready for the man. After struggling upward, pulling at rocks and vines, he pushed the man out, and with his last strength, crawled out himself.
>
> The man looked around, very happy to be out of the hole. The gorilla lay beside him, panting. The man said, "Thank you, Gorilla. Can you guide me out of this forest?" The gorilla replied, "Yes, Man, but first I must sleep for awhile to get my strength back."
>
> As the gorilla slept, the man watched him and began to think: "I

Hate is never conquered by hate. Hate is conquered by love. This is an eternal law.
—The Dhammapada

am very hungry. I can find my way out of this forest on my own. This is just an animal. I could drop one of these boulders on its head, kill it, and eat it. Why don't I do that?"

So the man lifted up one of the boulders as high as he could, and threw it down hard on the gorilla's head. The gorilla cried out in pain and sat up quickly, stunned by the blow, blood pouring down his face. As the gorilla looked at the man and realized what had happened, tears gathered in his eyes. He shook his head in sorrow and said, "Poor Man. Now you'll never *be happy."*

Reflections on Goodwill and Ill Will

This story has always touched me deeply. It gives us a lot to think about:

- Goodwill and ill will are about intention: the *will* is for good or ill. The gorilla intended to be helpful, and the man intended to kill.

- These intentions are expressed through action and inaction, word and deed, and—especially—thoughts. How do you feel when you sense another person taking potshots at you in her mind? What does it feel like to take potshots of your own? Ill will plays a lot of mini-movies in the simulator, those little grumbling stories about other people. Remember: while the movie is running, your neurons are wiring together.

- Ill will tries to justify itself: *This is just an animal.* In the moment, the rationalizations sound plausible, like the whisperings of Wormtongue in *The Lord of the Rings*. Only later do we realize how we have tricked ourselves.

- The gorilla's loving-kindness was its own reward. He was not burdened with anger or hatred. The first dart landed in the form of a boulder; there was no need to add insult to injury with a second dart of ill will.

- No need either, for the gorilla to seek retribution. He knew that the man would never be happy as a result of his actions. Stephen Gaskin (2005) describes karma as hitting golf balls in a shower. Often our attempts at payback just get in the way of balls already ricocheting back toward the person who sent them flying in the first place.

- Letting go of ill will does not mean passivity, silence, or allowing yourself or others to be harmed. The gorilla was not cowed by the man, and he named what was there to be named. There is plenty of room for speaking truth to power and for effective action without succumbing to ill will. Think of Mahatma Ghandi or Martin Luther King, Jr. In fact, with a clear mind and a peaceful heart, your actions are likely to be more effective.

Taming the Wolf of Hate

Here are numerous methods for cultivating goodwill and abandoning ill will. You'll be naturally drawn to some more than others. The point isn't to do all of them, but to know that you have lots of different ways to tame the wolf of hate.

CULTIVATE POSITIVE EMOTIONS

In general, really nourish and develop positive emotions such as happiness, contentment, and peacefulness. For example, look for things to be happy about, and take in the good whenever possible. Positive feelings calm the body, quiet the mind, create a buffer against stress, and foster supportive relationships—all of which reduce ill will.

BE AWARE OF THE PRIMING

Be mindful of factors that stimulate your sympathetic nervous system—such as stress, pain, worry, or hunger—and thus prime you for ill will. Try to defuse this priming early on: eat dinner before talking, take a shower, read something inspiring, or talk with a friend.

PRACTICE NONCONTENTION

Don't argue unless you have to. Inside your own mind, try not to get swirled along by the mind-streams of other people. Reflect on the neurological turbulence underlying their thoughts: the incredibly complicated, dynamic, and largely arbitrary churning of momentary neural assemblies into coherence and then chaos. Getting upset about somebody's thoughts is like getting upset about spray from a waterfall. Try to decouple your thoughts from the other person's. Tell yourself: *She's over there and I'm over here. Her mind is separate from my mind.*

BE CAREFUL ABOUT ATTRIBUTING INTENTIONS

Be cautious about attributing intentions to other people. Prefrontal theory-of-mind networks attribute intentions routinely, but they are often wrong. Most of the time you are just a bit player in other people's dramas; they are not targeting you in particular. Consider this parable from the Taoist teacher, Chuang Tzu (which I've updated):

Imagine that you are relaxing in a canoe on a river, when suddenly there is a hard thump against the side of it, dumping you into the water. You come up sputtering, and see that two teenagers with snorkels have snuck up and tipped you over. How do you feel?

Next imagine that everything is the same—the canoe, the sudden dumping into the river—except this time when you come up sputtering, you see that a huge submerged log has drifted downstream and smacked into your canoe. Now how do you feel?

For most people, the second scenario doesn't feel as bad: the first dart still landed (you're dumped in the river), but there is no need for second darts in the form of hurt and anger from feeling picked on personally. Truly, many people are like logs: it's wise to get out of their way if you can—or reduce the impact—but they're not *aiming* at you. Consider, too, the many factors upstream that have led them to do whatever they've done (see the Ten Thousand Things exercise).

The Ten Thousand Things

Do this exercise at whatever pace you like, with your eyes open or closed.

Relax and steady the mind, focusing on the breath.

Pick a situation in which you feel someone has wronged you. Be mindful of your reactions to this person, especially the deeper ones. Scan yourself for any ill will.

Now reflect on some of the various causes—the ten thousand things— that have led this person to act in the way that he has.

Consider biologically based factors affecting him, like pain, age, innate temperament, or intelligence.

Consider the realities of his life: race, gender, class, job, responsibilities, daily stresses.

Consider whatever you know about his childhood. Consider major events in his life as an adult.

> *Consider his mental processes, personality, values, fears, hot buttons, hopes, and dreams.*
>
> *Consider his parents in light of whatever you know or can reasonably guess about them; consider, too, the factors that may have shaped their lives.*
>
> *Reflect on the historical events and other upstream forces that have formed the river of causes flowing through his life today.*
>
> *Look inside yourself again. Do you feel any differently now about him? Do you feel any differently about yourself?*

BRING COMPASSION TO YOURSELF

As soon as you feel mistreated, bring compassion to yourself—this is urgent care for the heart. Try putting your hand on your cheek or heart to stimulate the embodied experience of receiving compassion.

INVESTIGATE THE TRIGGERS

Inspect the underlying trigger of your ill will, such as a sense of threat or alarm. Look at it realistically. Are you exaggerating what happened in any way? Are you focusing on a single negative thing amidst a dozen good ones?

PUT THINGS IN PERSPECTIVE

Put whatever happened in perspective. The effects of most events fade with time. They're also part of a larger whole, the great majority of which is usually fine.

PRACTICE GENEROSITY

Use things that aggravate you as a way to practice generosity. Consider letting people have what they took: their victory, their bit of money or time, their one-upping. Be generous with forbearance and patience.

REGARD ILL WILL AS AN AFFLICTION

Approach your own ill will as an affliction upon *yourself* so that you'll be motivated to drop it. Ill will feels bad and has negative health consequences; for example, regular hostility increases the risk of cardiovascular disease. Your ill will always harms you, but often it has no effect on the other person; as they say in twelve-step programs: *Resentment is when I take poison and wait for you to die.*

STUDY ILL WILL

Take a day and really examine even the least bit of ill will you experience. See what causes it and what its effects are.

SETTLE INTO AWARENESS

Settle into awareness, observing ill will but not identifying with it, watching it arise and disappear like any other experience.

ACCEPT THE WOUND

Life includes getting wounded. Accept as a fact that people will sometimes mistreat you, whether accidentally or deliberately. Of course, this doesn't mean enabling others to harm you, or failing to assert yourself. You're just accepting the facts on the ground. Feel the hurt, the anger, the fear, but let them flow through you. Ill will can become a way to avoid facing your deep feelings and pain.

RELAX THE SENSE OF SELF

Relax the sense of self. Experiment with letting go of the idea that there was actually an "I" or "me" who was affronted or wounded (see chapter 13).

MEET MISTREATMENT WITH LOVING-KINDNESS

Traditionally, loving-kindness is considered the direct antidote to ill will, so resolve to meet mistreatment with loving-kindness. No matter what. A famous sutra in Buddhism sets a high standard: "Even if bandits were to sever you savagely limb by limb with a two-handled saw...you should train thus: 'Our minds will remain unaffected, and we shall utter no evil words; we shall abide compassionate for their welfare, with a mind of loving-kindness, without inner hate'" (Nanamoli and Bodhi 1995, 223).

Personally, I'm not there yet, but if it's possible to stay loving while being horribly mistreated—and from some of the accounts of people in awful circumstances, it clearly is—then we should be able to rise up in lesser situations, like getting cut off in traffic or being put down yet again by a teenager.

COMMUNICATE

To the extent that it's useful, speak your truth and stick up for yourself with skillful assertiveness. Your ill will is telling you something. The art is to understand its message—perhaps that another person is not a true friend, or that you need to be clearer about your boundaries—without being swept away by anger.

HAVE FAITH IN JUSTICE

As in the story of the gorilla above, have faith that others will pay their own price one day for what they've done. You don't have to be the justice system.

DON'T TEACH LESSONS IN ANGER

Realize that some people won't get the lesson no matter how much you try. So why create problems for yourself in a pointless effort to teach them?

FORGIVE

Forgiveness doesn't mean changing your view that wrongs have been done. But it does mean letting go of the emotional charge around feeling wronged. The greatest beneficiary of your forgiveness is usually you. (For more on this subject, see *The Art of Forgiveness, Lovingkindness, and Peace* by Jack Kornfield and *Forgive for Good* by Fred Luskin.)

LOVING-KINDNESS FOR THE WHOLE WORLD

In light of our ancient tendency to collapse the field of love to a small circle of "us" surrounded by "them," it's good to cultivate the habit of pushing that circle out—widening it ultimately to include the whole world. Here are some suggestions for doing so.

Expanding the Category of "Us"

Be mindful of the automatic mental processes that cause you to identify with a particular group (e.g., gender, race, religion, sexual orientation, political party, nation), and then regard members of different groups as *others*. Focus on similarities between "us" and "them," not differences. Recognize that everything is connected to everything else, that "us" is the whole wide world—that, in a deep sense, the entire planet is your home and the people on it is are your extended family. Deliberately create mental categories that include you along with people you usually regard as not-me; for example, when you see someone in a wheelchair, think about how we are all disabled in one way or another.

Be particularly mindful of the default processes of valuing your own group while devaluing others (Efferson, Lalive, and Feh 2008). Notice how often that valuing actually has no rational basis. Be aware of the little ways that your mind regards others as less of a person than you—as an "It" to your "I." Focus on the good things about people in other groups. Regard people more as individuals than as representatives of a group, which reduces prejudice (Fiske 2002).

Reducing the Sense of Threat

Be mindful of any sense of threat. This feeling evolved to protect us in environments that were much more dangerous than anything most of us face today. In reality, how likely is it that other people will actually harm you?

Mutual Benefit

Look for opportunities for cooperative exchanges with members of other groups (e.g., sharing child care, doing business). When people depend on each other for their welfare, and come to experience each other as reliable and honorable, it's a lot harder to see each other as enemies.

Warming the Heart

Reflect on the suffering so many people endure. Reflect, too, on what others may have been like as young children—this will activate the warmth and goodwill we naturally feel toward little kids.

Remember the feeling you get around someone who loves you, which stimulates your capacities to care about others. Next, call to mind the experience of really caring about someone who is an "us" to you; that primes your neural circuits to care about someone who could be a "them." Then extend the sense of "us" to include every living being on our planet—as in the meditation on loving-kindness on the next page.

A Meditation on Loving-Kindness

Here is an extended meditation on loving-kindness:

Find a posture that helps you remain relaxed and alert. Settle into the breath. Establish some equanimity, some mental spaciousness and balance.

Be aware of the sensations of the breath in the region of the heart. Bring to mind the feeling of being with someone you love.

Keep feeling that love. Sense that love flowing through your heart, perhaps in a rhythm with the breath. Feel how that love has a life of its own, flowing through your heart, not specific to any one person.

Sense your love toward the people you know well, your friends and family. Feel a generous loving-kindness flowing through your heart in rhythm with the breath.

Feel that loving-kindness extending farther outward, toward the many people you know who are neutral to you. Wish them the best, too. Wish that they suffer less. That they be truly happy.

You may sense this loving-kindness like a warmth or light. Or like a spreading pool, with gentle waves extending farther and farther to include ever more people.

Feel your loving-kindness reaching out to include even difficult people; your loving-kindness has a life and a strength of its own. Your loving-kindness understands that many factors affected these difficult people and led them to be a problem for you. You wish that even people who have mistreated you may suffer less. That they, too, may be truly happy.

The peacefulness and strength of this loving-kindness flows outward ever farther to include people who you know exist, though you do not know them personally. Sense loving-kindness for all the people living in your country today, whether you agree with them or not, whether you like them or not.

Take a few minutes to explore extending your loving-kindness to the billions of people living here on earth. Loving-kindness for someone somewhere laughing. Loving-kindness for someone crying. Loving-kindness for someone getting married. Loving-kindness for someone caring for a sick child or parent. Loving-kindness for someone worried. Loving-kindness for someone being born. Loving-kindness for someone dying.

Your loving-kindness is flowing comfortably, perhaps in rhythm with the breath. Your loving-kindness is extending to all living beings on this earth. Wishing them all well. All kinds of animals, in the sea, on the earth, in the air: may they all be healthy and at ease. Wishing well to plants of all kinds: may they all be healthy and at ease. Wishing well to microorganisms of all kinds, the amoebas, the bacteria, even the viruses: may every living being be at ease.

So that all beings are "us."

So that all children are my own.

All life, my relatives.

The whole earth, my home.

Chapter 10: KEY POINTS

🪷 If compassion is the wish that someone not suffer, kindness is the wish that he or she be happy. It has a loving quality to it, thus the term "loving-kindness." When you practice kindness, you tame the wolf of hate and nurture the wolf of love.

🪷 There are many ways to do this; they include forming the intention to be kind, translating this intention into specific good wishes, meditating on loving-kindness, focusing on kindness in daily life, and using love itself as a path of practice.

🪷 It's easy to be kind when others treat you well. The challenge is to preserve your loving-kindness when they treat you badly—to preserve goodwill in the face of ill will.

🪷 It helps to remember that kindness is its own reward, that consequences often come to others without you needing to bring justice to them yourself, and that you can be assertive without falling into ill will.

🪷 There are many ways to turn ill will to goodwill and tame the wolf of hate. Be careful about the intentions you attribute to others; take fewer things personally; regard your ill will as an affliction upon yourself that you naturally want to be relieved of; resolve to meet mistreatment with loving-kindness; communicate and assert yourself; and forgive.

🪷 Extend the circle of "us" to include as much of the world as you possibly can. Be mindful of automatic categorizations into "us" and "them" and look for ways that "them" is actually "us"; notice whenever you feel threatened, and consider whether there are actually any threats; consciously warm your heart toward others; practice loving-kindness for the whole world.

Part Four

Wisdom

chapter 11

Foundations of Mindfulness

The education of attention would be
an education par excellence.

—William James

We hear the word "mindful" more and more these days, but what does it actually mean? Being mindful simply means having good control over your attention: you can place your attention wherever you want and it stays there; when you want to shift it to something else, you can.

When your attention is steady, so is your mind: not rattled or hijacked by whatever pops into awareness, but stably present, grounded, and unshakeable. Attention is like a spotlight, and what it illuminates streams into your mind and shapes your brain. Consequently, developing greater control over your attention is perhaps the single most powerful way to reshape your brain and thus your mind.

You can train and strengthen your attention just like any other mental ability (Jha, Krompinger, and Baime 2007; Tang et al. 2007); this chapter and the next one will show you many ways to do this. Let's start by exploring *how* your brain pays attention.

YOUR MINDFUL BRAIN

To help an animal survive—especially a complicated animal like us—the brain manages the flow of attention by balancing three needs: keeping information in mind, changing the contents of awareness, and finding the right amount of stimulation.

Holding onto Information

The brain must be able to keep important information in the foreground of awareness—such as a suspicious movement in the grass of the African savannah 100,000 years ago, or a phone number you just heard. My dissertation advisor, Bernard Baars (1997), developed the influential theory of a *global workspace of consciousness*— or in plainer terms, the mental chalkboard. Whatever you call it, it's a space that holds incoming information, old information retrieved from memory, and mental operations on both.

Updating Awareness

Second, your brain must routinely update this chalkboard with new information, whether it comes from the environment or from your own mind. For example, suppose you glimpse a familiar face across a crowded room but you just can't place it. When you finally recall the woman's name—Jane Smith, a friend of a friend—you update the image of her face with that information.

Seeking Stimulation

Third, your brain has a built-in desire for stimulation that likely evolved to prod our ancestors to keep seeking food, mates, and other resources. This need is so deep that in a sensory deprivation chamber (in which a person floats on warm salt water in a completely dark and silent space), the brain will sometimes start to hallucinate imagery just to have new information to process (Lilly 2006).

A Neural Balancing Act

Your brain continually juggles these three aspects of attention. Let's see how this works.

When you hold something in mind, such as a presentation at work or the sensations of breathing, the cortical regions that support working memory (a key component of the mental chalkboard) are relatively stable. To keep them this way, a kind of gate protects working memory from all of the other information coursing through the brain. When the gate is closed, you stay focused on one thing. When a new stimulus comes knocking—perhaps a startling thought, or the sound of a bird—the gate pops open, allowing new information in to update working memory. Then the gate closes behind it, keeping out other information. (Of course, it's actually more complicated than this; see Buschman and Miller 2007; Dehaene, Sergent, and Changeux 2003.)

As long as the contents of working memory are moderately stimulating, a steady stream of dopamine is produced, which keeps the gate closed. If the stimulation decreases significantly, the pulsing of dopamine-releasing neurons slows down, allowing the gate to open and new information to surge in. On the other hand, a spike in the rate of dopamine release—due to new opportunities or threats—will open the gate as well (Braver, Barch, and Cohen 2002; Cohen, Aston-Jones, and Gilzenrat 2005; O'Reilly 2006).

It's an ingeniously simple system that produces complex results. To use an example adapted from Todd Braver and Jonathan Cohen (2000), consider a monkey munching bananas in a tree. Steady eating maintains stable dopamine levels and keeps his focus on *this* tree. But when the bananas start to run out, rewards and thus dopamine levels drop, and thoughts about food in *that* tree now push into working memory. Or, if a friendly monkey swings onto a nearby branch, dopamine spikes from this fresh stimulus also pop open the gate to awareness.

This dopamine-driven system interacts with another neural system—based in the basal ganglia—that tries to balance the rewards of stimulation-seeking (new food! new mates!) with its risks (exposure to predators, rivals, and other hazards). The basal ganglia are a kind of "stimostat" that registers the stimulation coming through the senses or from within the mind itself. As long as the amount of stimulation remains above a certain threshold, there's no need to trigger stimulation-seeking. But when stimulation drops below this threshold, the basal ganglia signal your brain to get more *now*—and you find yourself being provocative in a boring conversation or lost in thought while meditating.

NEUROLOGICAL DIVERSITY

People vary a lot in their tendencies with regard to holding onto information, updating awareness, and seeking stimulation (see the following table). For example, the normal range of temperament includes both those who like a lot of novelty and excitement, and those who prefer predictability and quiet. People at the high or low end of this range often face challenges, especially in modern settings that require sustained attention to things that may not be that interesting (e.g., in schools or corporate offices). For instance, someone whose awareness is very easily updated—whose gate to working memory is propped wide open—has a hard time screening out irrelevant and distracting stimuli.

Whatever your innate inclinations may be, your attention is also influenced by your life experiences and culture. For example, contemporary Western culture strains and sometimes overwhelms the brain with more information than it evolved to handle on a routine basis. Our culture also habituates the brain to a hyper-rich stream of stimulation—consider video games and shopping malls—so that a drop in this stream can feel dull and boring. Essentially, modern life takes the jumpy, distractible "monkey mind" we all started with and feeds it steroids. Against this backdrop, other factors—such as motivation, fatigue, low blood sugar, illness, anxiety, or depression—can also affect your attention.

The Results of Different Tendencies in the Three Aspects of Attention

Tendency Regarding Aspect of Attention	Aspect of Attention, and Its Results		
	Holding onto Information	Updating Awareness	Seeking Stimulation
High	Obsessiveness "Over-focusing"	Porous filters Distractibility Sensory overload	Hyperactivity Thrill-seeking
Moderate	Good concentration Ability to divide attention	Mental flexibility Assimilation Accommodation	Enthusiasm Adaptability
Low	Concentration fatigue Small working memory	Fixed views Obliviousness Flat learning curve	Stuckness Apathy Lethargy

What's Your Personal Profile?

Each of us has a personal profile of attentional capacities, shaped by temperament, life experiences, cultural influences, and other factors. Taken as a whole, what are the strengths and weaknesses of your attention? What would you like to improve?

One pitfall is ignoring this profile—or worse, being ashamed of it—and then trying to fit your personal square peg into the generic round hole. Another pitfall is never challenging your tendencies. Between these is a middle way in which you both adapt your work, family situation, and spiritual practices to your own nature, and you develop better control of your attention over time.

Individualize Your Approach

To use contemplative practice as an example, many traditional methods were developed in times and cultures that had relatively low stimulation levels. But what about people today who are used to much more stimulation, particularly those at the spirited end of the normal range of temperament? I've seen people like this give up on meditation because they just couldn't find a way to do it that would fit with their own brain.

In terms of its innate effects—distinct from how others react to a person—*neurological diversity* is much more significant than variations of gender, race, or sexual orientation. If contemplative traditions are to increase the diversity of their practitioners, they need to find more ways to welcome diverse kinds of brains. Further, here in the West, we particularly need to individualize contemplative practices because there is a premium—in busy, "householder" lives—on methods that are targeted, efficient, and effective.

Whether you want to be more focused at work, while talking with your partner, or during meditation, give yourself permission to adapt your approach to your own nature. Be compassionate about your personal challenges to mindfulness: they are not your fault, and the positive emotion of compassion could increase dopamine levels and help steady your mind.

Next, consider which of the three aspects of attention is most challenging for you: holding something in awareness, filtering out distractions, or managing the desire for stimulation. For example: Do you get tired quickly when you try to concentrate? Do you seem to have porous filters, so that you get distracted by many of the sights and sounds around you? Or are you the sort of person who needs a rich diet of stimulation? (Or some combination of these?)

For the rest of this chapter, we'll explore general-purpose methods for gaining greater control over your attention. Then, in the next chapter, we'll use the preeminent training in mindfulness—meditation—to improve your personal profile of attention abilities.

SET INTENTIONS

Use the power of your prefrontal cortex to set intentions to be more mindful:

- Establish a deliberate intention at the beginning of any activity that requires focus. Use statements such as *May my mind be steady.* Or just call up a silent feeling of determination.

- Get a bodily sense of being someone you know who is extremely focused. That uses the empathy systems in the brain to simulate within yourself the mindful nature of that other person.

- Keep reestablishing your intentions. For example, if you're in a meeting, every few minutes you could resolve anew to stay focused. One of my friends uses a little device that can be set to vibrate at different intervals; he leaves it in his pocket and gets a discrete wake-up call every ten minutes.

- Make the intention to be attentive the default setting of your life by developing the habit of everyday mindfulness.

Supports for Everyday Mindfulness

- Slow down.

- Talk less.

- When you can, do just one thing at a time. Reduce multitasking.

- Focus on your breath while doing daily activities.

- Relax into a feeling of calm presence with other people.

- Use routine events—such as the phone ringing, going to the bathroom, or drinking water—as "temple bells" to return you to a sense of centeredness.

- At meals, take a moment to reflect on where your food came from. For example, if you were focusing on the wheat in a slice of bread, you could imagine it growing in the fields and being harvested, threshed, stored, ground into flour, baked into loaves, and shipped to a market, all before arriving on your plate. You can go pretty far with this in just a few seconds. You might also imagine some of the people who helped turn this wheat into your bread, and the equipment and technology involved, as well as our ancient ancestors who slowly figured out how to domesticate wild grains.

- Simplify your life; give up lesser pleasures for greater ones.

STAY AWAKE AND ALERT

The brain can't be fully attentive unless it's fully awake. Unfortunately, the average person is sleep-deprived, getting about an hour less sleep a day than the body really needs. Try to get enough sleep ("enough" depends on your nature and factors such as fatigue, illness, thyroid problems, or depression). In other words, take care of yourself. Struggling to pay attention when you're tired is like spurring an exhausted horse to keep running uphill.

Presuming you're reasonably rested, several additional factors can increase your alertness:

• Sitting in an erect posture provides internal feedback to the *reticular formation*—a mesh-like network of nerves in the brain stem which is involved with wakefulness and consciousness—telling it that you need to stay vigilant and alert. This is a neurological reason behind a schoolteacher's demands to "sit up straight, class!" as well as the classic meditation instruction to sit upright in a dignified way.

• "Brighten the mind" is a traditional phrase used to describe infusing your awareness with energy and clarity. In fact, to overcome drowsiness, it's sometimes suggested that you literally visualize light. Neurologically, this "brightening" likely involves a surge of norepinephrine throughout the brain; that neurotransmitter—also triggered by the stress-response cascade—is a general orienting signal that fosters alertness.

• Oxygen is to the nervous system what gasoline is to your car. Although just 2 percent of body weight, your brain uses roughly 20 percent of your oxygen. By taking several deep breaths, you increase oxygen saturation in your blood and thus rev up your brain.

QUIET THE MIND

When the mind is quiet, fewer things bubble up to distract you and it's easier to remain mindful. In chapter 5 we explored ways to "cool the fires"; these help quiet the mind through relaxing the body and calming emotions and desires. The methods here focus on stilling the clamor of verbal thought—that endlessly nattering voice in the back of the head.

Be Aware of the Body as a Whole

Some parts of the brain are linked by *reciprocal inhibition*: when one part activates, it suppresses another one. To some extent, the left and right hemispheres have this relationship; thus, when you stimulate the right hemisphere by engaging the activities it specializes in, the verbal centers of the left hemisphere are effectively shushed.

The right, visual-spatial hemisphere has the greater responsibility for representing the state of your body, so awareness of the body can help suppress left-brain verbal chatter. Right hemisphere activation increases further when you sense the body as a *whole*, which draws upon the global, gestalt processing of that hemisphere.

To practice awareness of the whole body, start with the breath as a whole; rather than allow attention to move as it normally does, from sensation to sensation, try to experience your breath as a single, unified gestalt of sensations in your belly, chest, throat, and nose. It's normal for this unified gestalt sensing to crumble after a second or two; when it does, just try to recreate it. Then expand awareness to include the body as a whole, sensed as a single perception, as one whole thing. This sense of the body as a whole will also tend to crumble quickly, especially in the beginning; when it does, simply restore it again, if only for a few seconds. You'll get better at this with practice, and will even be able to do this in the middle of everyday settings such as meetings.

Besides its benefits for quieting the verbal mind, whole body awareness supports *singleness of mind*. This is a meditative state in which all aspects of experience come together as a whole and attention is very steady. As we'll see in the next chapter, this is one of the factors of deep contemplative absorption.

Hush the Verbal Centers

Send a gentle instruction to the verbal centers, something along the lines of *Hush, now, it's time to relax and be quiet. There's nothing important to talk about right now. You'll have plenty of time to talk later, throughout the rest of the day.* In doing so, you use the power of prefrontal intention to bias verbal activity toward relative quiet. When (not if, alas) the voices in the head start muttering again, repeat the instruction to them. For example: *It's not time for chatter, your yammering is a burden on me, you can talk after this meeting/ tax return/golf putt.* Alternately, you might occupy your brain's language centers with other verbal activities, such as repeating a favorite saying, mantra, or prayer in the back of your mind.

If you like, make an appointment with yourself to let your mind really yammer after you're done with the activity you're staying focused on. Be sure to keep this appointment—it's weirdly fun and definitely interesting to amp up the verbal stream in your mind; it helps you see how arbitrary and meaningless most of it is.

ABIDE AS AWARENESS ITSELF

As mindfulness stabilizes, you will rest more and more as awareness itself. Awareness contains *mind-objects*, a general term for any mental content, including perceptions, thoughts, desires, memories, emotions, and so on. Although mind-objects may dance busily with each other, awareness itself is never disturbed. Awareness is a kind of screen on which mind-objects register, like—in the Zen saying—

the reflections on a pond of geese flying overhead. But awareness is never sullied or rattled by the passing show.

In your brain, the neural patterns represented within awareness are highly variable, but the representational capacities themselves—the basis of the subjective experience of awareness—are generally very stable. Consequently, resting as awareness brings a beautiful sense of inner clarity and peace. These feelings are generally deepest in meditation, but you can cultivate a greater sense of abiding as awareness throughout the day. Use the following guided reflection to help you do just that.

Resting in Awareness

Relax, with your eyes open or closed. Settle into just being here, a peaceful body breathing. Observe the sensations of your breath coming and going. Establish a clear sense of observing as distinct from that which is observed.

Observe the flow of mind-objects without getting drawn into them; don't chase mental carrots or struggle with sticks. Have thoughts and so on, but don't be them: don't identify with the contents of awareness. Watch the movie without stepping into the screen.

Allow experiences to come and go without attempting to influence them. Likes and dislikes may arise regarding mind-objects; accept these preferences as just more mind-objects. See that all mind-objects have the same nature: they come and they go.

Settle into the present moment. Drop the past and let go of the future. Receive each moment without trying to connect one moment to the next. Abide as presence, neither remembering nor planning. There is no straining, no seeking for anything. Nothing to have, nothing to do, nothing to be.

Notice the gaps between mind-objects, a palpable way to discern the field of awareness distinct from its contents. For example, deliberately think a specific thought, such as "there is breathing," and then observe

---

what is present immediately before and after the thought. See that there is a kind of peaceful readiness, an unused capacity, a fertile vacancy.

Notice the spacelike qualities of awareness: it is boundless, still and silent, empty until something appears, vast enough to hold anything, always present and reliable, and never altered by the mind-objects passing through it like shooting stars. But do not mistake any concept of awareness—which is just another mind-object—for awareness itself. Keep returning to simply being, simply present, opening out to the infinite, without boundaries.

Gently explore other qualities of awareness; stay with your direct experience instead of conceptualizing about awareness. Is there a kind of luminosity to it? Does awareness have a subtle compassion? Are mind-objects simply modifications of awareness itself?

chapter 11: KEY POINTS

✤ What flows through your attention sculpts your brain. Therefore, controlling your attention may be the single most effective way to shape your brain, and thus your mind. You can train and strengthen attention like any other mental ability; mindfulness is well-controlled attention.

✤ Attention has three aspects to it: keeping information in awareness, updating awareness with new information, and seeking the right amount of stimulation.

✤ Information is held in working memory, which has a kind of dopamine-based gate. Steady stimulation keeps the gate closed. The gate gets opened by either a decrease or an increase in stimulation, which allows new information to surge into working memory, closing the gate behind it.

- 🪷 Additionally, the basal ganglia seek a certain amount of stimulation. If the stream of stimulation you're receiving is above that amount, all is well, but if the stream dries to a trickle, the basal ganglia signal other parts of the brain to find more stimulation.

- 🪷 There is a natural range of strengths and weaknesses with these three aspects of attention; this is one aspect of neurological diversity. Each person has his or her own profile. It's compassionate and sensible both to adapt your work, home life, and spiritual practices to your profile, and to improve your attention over time.

- 🪷 General-purpose ways to improve your attention include using intention, staying awake and alert, quieting the mind, and abiding as awareness.

chapter 12

Blissful Concentration

Penetrative insight joined with calm abiding
utterly eradicates afflicted states.

—Shantideva

Mindfulness brings insight and wisdom—and the best way to increase your mindfulness is through meditation. It's fine if you've never meditated before. In businesses, schools, and hospitals here and around the world, people are now learning meditative practices to become more productive, pay better attention, heal faster, and feel less stressed. We'll use meditation to explore multiple methods for training your attention; you can apply these methods to all sorts of nonmeditative situations as well.

THE POWER OF MEDITATION

The concentration that you gain from meditation takes the spotlight of attention and turns it into a laser beam. Concentration is the natural ally of insight, as you can see in this traditional Buddhist metaphor: *We find ourselves in a forest of ignorance and need a sharp machete to clear a path to liberating understanding; insight makes the blade sharp and concentration gives it power.* The deepest levels of contemplative concentration are valued in all traditions. For example, Buddhism's Eightfold Path includes Wise Concentration, which is about developing four highly focused states of mind called *jhanas*. (These usually take dedicated practice to enter; this chapter is not a how-to manual for the *jhanas*.)

The Challenges of Meditation

Meditation is a great way to pressure test your attention in order to strengthen it—precisely because it goes against the grain of the tendencies we evolved to survive.

Consider *focused attention* practices, in which you become absorbed in some object, such as the breath. Animals that locked their attention onto one thing for many minutes in a row, screened everything else out, and dropped the need for stimulation—perhaps absorbed in the sunlight filtering through the leaves—wouldn't notice ominous slithers or shadows nearby, and thus wouldn't pass on their genes. *Monkey mind* is the traditional, critical term for skittish attention—but this is exactly what helped our ancestors stay alive.

Or consider *open awareness* meditation, where you practice choiceless awareness of whatever comes to mind without becoming engaged by it; this is equally contrary to our evolutionary nature. Sensations, emotions, desires, and other mind-objects are *supposed* to attract attention so you'll respond to them. Letting them roll by without hopping on board just isn't natural.

Appreciating these challenges will help bring some good humor and self-compassion to your efforts to meditate.

Five Factors of Concentration

For thousands of years, people have investigated how to strengthen attention in the laboratory of contemplative practice. For example, Buddhism has identified five key factors for steadying the mind:

- **Applied attention**—initial directing of attention to an object, such as the beginning of the breath

- **Sustained attention**—staying focused on the object of attention, such as remaining aware of an entire inhalation from beginning to end

- **Rapture**—intense interest in the object; sometimes experienced as a rush of blissful sensations

- **Joy**—gladdening of the heart that includes happiness, contentment, and tranquility

- **Singleness of mind**—unification of awareness in which everything is experienced as a whole; few thoughts; equanimity; a strong sense of being *present*

Building on the general supports for mindfulness covered in the previous chapter, let's explore how to develop the neural substrates of these five factors. With practice, concentration naturally deepens for most people (Lutz, Slager, et al. 2008). Whether you're new to meditation or it's already an important part of your life, it's great to know that there really are things you can do inside your brain to steady your mind, even all the way to deep meditative absorption.

For simplicity, we'll refer to sitting meditation focused on the breath, but you can adapt these suggestions to other practices (e.g., yoga, chanting) and to other objects of attention (e.g., a mantra, loving-kindness). As your mind becomes steadier, bring this stability and focus to other types of contemplative practice (e.g., insight meditation, prayer, investigation of impermanence) and to everyday activities.

The next three sections address applied and sustained attention, and the different weaknesses people have with these. After that, we'll explore rapture and joy, and then singleness of mind. We'll conclude with a guided meditation that pulls together all five factors.

KEEPING ATTENTION ON ITS OBJECT

These suggestions will deepen your engagement with the contents of awareness and thus help keep closed the gate to working memory (discussed in the previous chapter):

- Imagine a little guardian who watches how well you are watching the breath and gives your attention a boost if it starts to flag. This guardian "lives" mainly in the anterior cingulate cortex (ACC), which compares actual performance with a goal; the ACC is the part of your brain that's most involved in applying and sustaining attention.

- Draw on the language centers of your brain through counting or noting the breath. For example, softly, in the back of your mind, count each breath from 1 to 10 and then start over. If you lose track, just begin again with 1. (You can also count down, from 10 to 1, starting over with 10 if you lose track.) If you're ambitious, aim for ten sets of ten breaths counted, a hundred in all without losing track; if you like, start with your hands closed, straightening out a finger for each set of ten. This can be a great way to start a meditation, bringing your mind to a settled place quite quickly.

- Alternately, gently note your experience—for example, thinking "in, out" for each breath. If it helps, softly note other mind-objects: "thinking," "memory," "worrying," "planning," and so on.

- Deepen your involvement with the breath through bringing warmth, fondness, and even devotion to it. Emotions for something naturally intensify attention toward it, plus they engage the brain as a whole; consequently, more neural networks are involved with the object of attention.

FILTERING OUT DISTRACTIONS

Here are some ways to preserve a relatively quiet space in your mind by keeping out distracting intruders:

- Take a few minutes at the start of meditation to open up to and explore the sounds and other stimuli around you; do the same with your inner world. Paradoxically, inviting distractions *in* encourages them to move *out*. Dropping the second dart of resistance to them reduces the amount of attention they get. Additionally, the brain tends to become habituated to a steady stimulus and stops noticing it after a while.

- Also, receiving something completely often helps it to pass through the mind more quickly. It's like people knocking on your door: if you ignore them, they keep at it, but when you open the door, they come in, say their piece, and usually leave. You can help them on their way by using the soft noting technique described above (e.g., "traffic noises...irritation"). Allowing something to emerge fully in awareness enables its latent pattern of neural activity to emerge fully as well. Message now delivered, that neural coalition no longer needs to press forward, no longer needs to compete with other coalitions for center stage. And, having arrived and made its communication, it will now be subject to the powerful processes that keep trying to update working memory—

which will usually wipe the mental chalkboard clean after a while in order to make way for a new coalition.

- After the sense of distraction has diminished, refocus on your object of attention (or on whatever meditation you're doing). If distractions return, you can always open to them again for a few minutes.

- Alternatively, gently bat away distracting thoughts at the earliest stages of their development and keep falling back into your breath. You are disrupting the formation of neural coalitions before they completely consolidate.

- Remind yourself that you can think about other things later; tell yourself you've made an appointment to meditate and you have to keep it. This uses the capacity of the prefrontal cortex to exert top-down influence over the stream of perception and thought (Engel, Fries, and Singer 2001).

- Observe how everything moving through the mind is a passing show, with transient performers endlessly bumped off the stage by new ones. Why get caught up with one thing when you know it'll soon be replaced by something else?

- If all else fails, make the distraction itself the object of attention for this meditation period. One time, when I was trying to concentrate on the breath, I kept being distracted by a loud air conditioner. After a while, I gave up and switched to that sound—and gradually became pretty absorbed in it.

MANAGING THE DESIRE FOR STIMULATION

The following methods increase the stimulation of meditation, and they're particularly useful for people with a spirited temperament. The art is to use them only as long as they're needed to steady the mind, not as an escape from the discipline of meditation.

- The brain intensifies attention in response to novelty. So notice the individual qualities of each breath. Draw in new information by paying attention to details, such as the sensations at different spots on the upper lip.

- Focus on multiple sensations in a large area of your body, such as the chest. Or notice how breathing creates sensations all over your body, such as subtle movements in your hips and head.

- Break the breath into small parts so there's more to notice. Inhalation, exhalation, and the little pause in between—that's three parts right there. Or divide each inhalation and exhalation further. (You can apply similar methods to walking meditation and other practices.)

- Do walking meditation, which provides more stimulation than sitting quietly. Or use related practices for meditation, such as yoga or tai chi.

- Open to feelings of sufficiency and contentment. This both increases stimulation and conveys the message that you are full as you are and don't need to reach for anything else.

- Since the neutral feeling tone is not stimulating, it prompts the mind to go scurrying off looking for action. So watch what your mind does with neutral mind-objects, and increase their stimulation by softly noting "neutral."

RAPTURE AND JOY

Now let's explore the next two factors of absorption: rapture and joy. Positive feelings like these help concentrate attention by causing steadily high transmissions of dopamine to the neural substrate of working memory. As we saw in the previous chapter, the gate to working memory—and thus to the field of awareness—pops open both when dopamine slumps and when it spikes. Steadily high dopamine—like from positive feelings—prevents slumps. Further, when dopamine-releasing neurons are already near their peak firing rate, it's hard to get a spike—they're near their ceiling and can't get much higher. Thus, the more enjoyable and intense your feelings are, the greater the dopamine release—and the more concentrated your attention.

In other words, whether you are going deep into meditative contemplation or just trying to keep your eyes open in an afternoon meeting, happiness can really help. Personally, I have found the intensification of positive emotions during meditation to be a wonderful practice: it feels great, it increases concentration, and it nourishes a strong feeling of well-being throughout the day.

Here are some ways to intensify rapture and joy. Try them first in your meditation, and then experiment with them in everyday situations.

- Notice rapture and joy when they emerge on their own. Open to them and invite them in.

- Think to yourself: *May rapture (bliss) arise. May joy (happiness, contentment, tranquility) arise.* In a relaxed way, intend for rapture and joy to arise.

- Integrate rapture and joy with the sensations of the breath. Let bliss breathe you, let the breath be tranquil.

- Make rapture or joy the new object of your attention, and then become increasingly absorbed in that state of being.

- Joy encompasses happiness, contentment, and tranquility; explore each one of these. In particular, tranquility is one of the seven factors of enlightenment in Buddhism, and it also leads to concentration. This sense of great peace and quiet—like a still, glassy pond—is really worth knowing and cultivating.

- Be mindful of the nuances of rapture, happiness, contentment, and tranquility. Get a clear sense of each state so you can call it to mind in the future. Over time, it is natural for a person to be drawn increasingly away from the intensity of rapture toward the subtler but more sublime rewards of happiness, contentment, and tranquility.

- Experiment with gently intensifying these states of mind, perhaps in concert with a subtle quickening of the breath. There is a natural rhythm in which a state gets stronger for seconds, maybe minutes, and then settles back down—and then you can intensify it again.

- Over the course of your meditation, it often works to move from rapture to happiness to contentment to tranquility. Then, as the meditation approaches its end, reverse the journey step by step rather than hopping straight from tranquility to rapture.

- In general, find the sweet spot where you are just active enough inside your mind to encourage these various states, but you're not overdirecting your mind or attached to any particular result.

SINGLENESS OF MIND

Singleness of mind involves the unification of awareness, grounded in a deepening absorption in the object of attention. Thoughts are minimal and the mind is very steady. You feel very present, with a growing sense of equanimity.

> *If there is no stillness, there is no silence.*
>
> *If there is no silence, there is no insight.*
>
> *If there is no insight, there is no clarity.*
>
> —Tenzin Priyadarshi

This state is probably associated with the high-frequency gamma waves that are seen in experienced meditators (Lutz et al. 2004). As a person goes deeper into meditation, there appears to be both a spreading and a strengthening of gamma wave activity, which presumably underlies the experience of a growing spaciousness and stability of awareness.

Singleness of mind tends to follow naturally from the other four factors of concentration. You can also encourage it in several additional ways. First, as we discussed earlier, whole body awareness stimulates the holistic, gestalt processing of the right hemisphere, and thus helps unify the mind. To experience whole body awareness, start by getting a sense of the breathing as a whole, and then extend that sensing to include the body as one unified whole; if the experience crumbles, just keep regenerating it until it's more stable. Second, give yourself over to the present moment as it is. Drop the past and the future; for this time, in this meditation, renounce worrying, planning, or fantasizing. Nurture a continuity of here-and-now presence. Third, relax the sense of personal self as much as you can (we'll explore this further in the next chapter). Too much "I" will just distract and divide you from the beautiful depth of being that is singleness.

CONCENTRATION MEDITATION

No matter where you start, you can become better at concentration. It's like a muscle: when you use it, it gets stronger. When your mind wanders, as it inevitably will, try not to be self-critical; simply return to awareness of the next breath. As the Buddhist teacher Joseph Goldstein says, be relaxed but not casual. It's not what happened in the past that matters but what you do *now*. You can always reapply your attention to the breath and sustain it. You can always open to rapture and joy. And you can always tip farther into singleness of mind.

The Buddha offered a kind of road map for contemplative practice: steady the mind, quiet it, bring it to singleness, and concentrate it. We'll use this as a guide for the following meditation, which draws on the supports for mindfulness and concentration covered in this chapter and previous ones. You can also adapt these instructions for other meditations or mindfulness activities.

The Meditation

Find a comfortable posture, one that is both relaxed and alert. Close your eyes or leave them open, gazing a few feet in front of you.

Be aware of sounds coming and going. Aware of sensations in your body. Aware of thoughts and feelings. Notice anything that is particularly distracting; be mindful of this distraction for a while and then see if you can shift your focus to the breath.

Form an intention for your meditation, perhaps with words or perhaps wordlessly. Imagine being someone very focused, either a person you know or a historical figure like the Buddha.

Really relax. Take a big inhalation and then exhale fully, feeling the tension leave your body. Be aware of the internal sensations of breathing, cool air coming in and warm air going out, the chest and belly rising and falling. Don't try to control the breath in any way, just let it be what it is. Stay aware of the breath throughout the meditation, using it as a kind of anchor.

Feel as safe as you can. You're in a protected setting, strong in yourself, able to relax vigilance and bring attention inward.

Find some compassion for yourself. Bring to mind other positive feelings as well, including soft ones such as gratitude.

Sense the benefits of this meditation sinking into you, nurturing and helping you, gently inclining your mind and brain in an ever more wholesome direction.

All right. For the next five minutes or more, try to stay present with each individual breath from beginning to end. Imagine a little guardian in your mind who is watching your attention and will let you know right away if it starts to wander. Give yourself over to each breath and abandon everything else. Let go of the past, let go of the future, and be present with each breath.

Find a place where the physical sensations of breathing are prominent, such as the chest or upper lip. At the beginning of each inhalation, apply attention to these sensations. Then sustain attention to them from beginning to end. Be aware of the space between inhalation and exhalation. Then apply attention to the exhalation and sustain attention to it all the way to its end.

If it helps, count each breath gently in your mind, from one to ten, starting over if you lose track. Or softly note the breath, "In, out." As concentration deepens, let these words fall away.

Give yourself over to the breath, renouncing all else during this meditation. Know the sensations in each breath. Breathing in, know that you are breathing in. Breathing out, know that you are breathing out.

All right. Be aware of any feelings of rapture or joy. Open to them and invite them in. May bliss arise. May happiness arise. Shift your attention to them for a while. As you can, intensify feelings of rapture and joy. Perhaps breathe a little faster. If you experience them, allow rushes of bliss to move through your body.

Let yourself feel very happy, very content, very tranquil. Explore the distinct qualities of rapture, happiness, contentment, and tranquility. Become increasingly absorbed in these states.

Bring rapture and joy into your breath, deepening your absorption further, really steadying your mind.

All right. Your mind is getting very quiet. Attention is absorbed mainly in one object, such as the sensations of the breath at the upper lip. Few verbal thoughts come, and they pass quickly. There's a great tranquility.

There's an awareness of breathing as a whole, all the sensations of the breath unified as a whole. Then an awareness of the body as a whole. Sense the whole body shifting slightly with the breath. You're not moving for or against anything passing through the mind. If something seems about to disturb the peace, let if pass and relax into the quiet.

All right. Your mind is coming into singleness. There is awareness of the body as a whole, of experience as a whole. Few thoughts, maybe none at all. A sense of boundaries and barriers falling away within your mind. No resistance to anything. Utterly letting go. Feel a growing unification spreading and strengthening in your mind. May singleness arise.

Allow states of mind to occur that may be unfamiliar in their fullness and profundity. Let go of any thoughts. Settle deeper into the breath, becoming one with the breath. Absorption in the breath is increasingly effortless. Nothing to reach for, nothing to be. Allow insight to arise, seeing into experience and the mind and the world. Little remnants of craving fall away. You're peaceful and free.

All right. When you like, gradually bring the meditation to an end. Gently return from wherever you are to tranquility, then contentment, then happiness, then a taste of rapture, then a more everyday state of mind. Take your time. Be gentle with yourself.

May this peacefulness and steadiness of mind sink into your being, becoming a part of you. May it nurture you and all those around you.

chapter 12: KEY POINTS

🪷 Mindfulness leads to wisdom, and the best way to increase mindfulness is meditation.

🪷 Besides its benefits for productivity, learning, and health, meditation concentrates the mind for contemplative practice; concentration supports deep and liberating insight into both the causes of suffering and the causes of great happiness and peace.

🪷 In Buddhism, there are five traditional factors that steady the mind: applied attention, sustained attention, rapture, joy, and singleness of mind. We explored many ways to strengthen their neural substrates.

🪷 We addressed difficulties with applied and sustained attention in terms of the three aspects of attention: holding onto its object, filtering out distractions, and managing the desire for stimulation.

🪷 Rapture and joy help concentrate attention by causing steadily high transmissions of dopamine; these keep the gate to working memory shut so you can become increasingly absorbed with what's inside.

🪷 Singleness of mind is probably supported by fast gamma wave synchronization of large areas of the brain. You can encourage this state through the other four factors of concentration, plus whole body awareness, surrendering to the moment, and relaxing the sense of self.

chapter 13

Relaxing the Self

To study the Way is to study the self.
To study the self is to forget the self.
To forget the self is to be enlightened by all things.

—Dogen

Now we come to perhaps the single greatest source of suffering—and therefore to what it's most important to be wise about: the apparent self.

Look into your own experience. When you take things personally—or hunger for approval—what happens? You suffer. When you identify with something as "me" or try to possess something as "mine," you set yourself up for suffering, since all things are frail and will inevitably pass away. When you stand apart from other people and the world as "I," you feel separate and vulnerable—and suffer.

On the other hand, when you relax the subtle sense of contraction at the very nub of "me"—when you're immersed in the flow of life rather than standing apart from it, when ego and egotism fade to the background—then you feel more peaceful and fulfilled. You may have experienced this under a starry night sky, at the edge of the sea, or when your child was born. Paradoxically, the less your "I" is here, the happier you are. Or, as both Buddhist monks and inmates on death row sometimes say: "No self, no problem."

At some point in life, we all ask the same question: *Who am I?* And no one really knows the answer. The self is a slippery subject—especially when it's the subject that is regarding itself as an object! So let's begin by grounding this airy topic with an experiential activity—taking the body for a walk. Then we'll investigate the nature of the self in your brain. Last, we'll explore methods for relaxing and releasing "self-ing" in order to feel more confident, peaceful, and joined with all things. (For more on this profound matter, which reaches beyond the scope of a single chapter, see *Living Dhamma* by Ajahn Chah, *The Book: On the Taboo Against Knowing Who You Are* by Alan Watts, *I Am That: Talks with Sri Nisargadatta Maharaj*, or *The Spiritual Teaching of Ramana Maharshi*.)

Taking the Body for a Walk

Try to do this exercise with as little sense of "I" as possible. If you become uncomfortable in any way, focus your attention on basic physical sensations, such as in your feet or hands.

Exercise

Relax. Be aware of your body breathing.

Establish the intention to let go of the self as much as you can, and see what that's like.

Be aware of breathing. Be breathing. There's nothing else to do. No need for the self to do anything.

Feel as safe as possible. Relax any sense of threat or aversion. No need to mobilize the self for protection.

Feel peacefulness rising and falling with each breath. No need for self to grasp at any pleasure.

Keep letting go. Let go with every exhalation. Let go of the self with every exhalation.

Relax any control of breathing. Let the body manage breathing, just like it does during sleep.

Breathing continues. Awareness continues. There is spacious awareness with little sense of self. Peaceful and pleasant, no need for self. Awareness and the world going on, doing all right without a self.

Slowly move the gaze around. Sights need no self to receive them.

Explore small movements, without a self directing them. A finger moves a little, weight shifts in the chair. Intentions prompt those movements, but no "I" needs to guide them.

Gently stand up without self guiding the standing. There is awareness of standing here, but does there need to be a self here?

Move a little while standing, perceptions and movements happening without needing an owner or director of those experiences.

Then explore walking about, slowly or quickly. Without needing self to do so. Perceptions and movements occurring without anyone identifying with those experiences. Take a few minutes for this.

After a while, sit down again. Rest in breathing, simply present, being aware. Thoughts about the self, or thoughts from the perspective of "I," are just contents of awareness like any other, not special in any way.

Relax and breathe. Sensations and feelings are just contents of awareness arising and dispersing. Self, too, arises and disperses in awareness, not a problem at all. Just self coming and going as it may. No problem at all.

Relax and breathe. See what's present when self is absent.

Relax and breathe. No problem at all.

Reflections

It may be a little hard to move back into the realm of verbal thought. While reading here, explore the sense of words comprehended without a self doing the comprehending. Notice that the mind can perform its functions just fine without a self in charge.

Looking back on the exercise:

- What was the experience of self, "I," or "mine?" What does self feel like? Is it a pleasant or unpleasant experience? Is there a sense of contraction when self increases?

- Is it possible to do many mental and physical activities without much sense of self?

- Was the self always the same, or did different aspects come to the forefront at different times? Did the intensity of the self change, too—was the sense of "I" sometimes strong and sometimes subtle?

- What led the self to change? What effects did fear or anger have, or other thoughts of threat? What effects did desire have, or other thoughts of opportunity? What effects did other people either encountered or imagined have? Does the self exist independently, or does it arise and change depending on causes and conditions?

SELF IN YOUR BRAIN

The experiences of self you just had—that it has many aspects, is just part of the whole person, is continually changing, and varies according to conditions—depend on the physical substrates of self in your brain. Thoughts, feelings, images, and so on exist as patterns of information represented by patterns of neural structure and activity. In the same way, the various aspects of the apparent self—and the intimate and powerful experience of *being* a self—exist as patterns in the mind and brain. The question is not whether those patterns exist. The key questions are: What is their *nature*? And does that which those patterns seem to stand for—an "I" who is the unified, ongoing owner of experiences and agent of actions—truly exist? Or is self like a unicorn, a mythical being whose representations exist but who is actually imaginary?

Self Has Many Aspects

The many aspects of self are based on structures and processes spread throughout the brain and nervous system, and embedded in the body's interactions with the world. Researchers categorize those aspects of self, and their neural underpinnings, in a variety of ways. For example, the *reflective self* ("I am solving a problem") likely arises mainly in neural connections among the anterior cingulate cortex, upper-outer prefrontal cortex (PFC), and hippocampus; the *emotional self* ("I am upset") emerges from the amygdala, hypothalamus, *striatum* (part of the basal ganglia), and upper brain stem (Lewis and Todd 2007). Different parts of your brain recognize your face in group photos, know about your personality, experience personal responsibility, and look at situations from your perspective rather than someone else's (Gillihan and Farah 2005).

The *autobiographical self* (D'Amasio 2000) incorporates the reflective self and some of the emotional self, and it provides the sense of "I" having a unique past and future. The *core self* involves an underlying and largely nonverbal feeling of "I" that has little sense of the past or the future. If the PFC—which provides most of the neural substrate of the autobiographical self—were to be damaged, the core self would remain, though with little sense of continuity with the past or future. On the other hand, if the subcortical and brain stem structures which the core self relies upon were damaged, then both the core and autobiographical selves would disappear, which suggests that the core self is the neural and mental foundation of the autobiographical self (D'Amasio 2000). When your mind is very quiet, the autobiographical self seems largely absent, which presumably corresponds to a relative deactivation of its neural substrate. Meditations that still the mind, such as the concentration practices we explored in the previous chapter, improve conscious control over that deactivation process.

The *self-as-object* arises when you deliberately think about yourself—"Would I rather eat Chinese or Italian food tonight? How come I'm so indecisive?"—or when associations to yourself spontaneously arise in awareness. These representations of "me" are contents within a narrative that strings together momentary snapshots of self into a kind of movie of a seemingly coherent self over time (Gallagher 2000). Narrative self-referencing relies on midline cortical structures (Farb et al. 2007), as well as on the junction of the temporal and parietal lobes, and on the back end of the temporal lobe (Legrand and Ruby 2009). These regions of your brain perform numerous other functions, too (e.g., thinking about other people, making evaluations), so they cannot be said to be specifically related to the self (Legrand and Ruby 2009). Representations of the self flit through them amidst all sorts of other mental contents, jostling together like different twigs and leaves in a stream, apparently without any neurologically special status.

More fundamentally, the *self-as-subject* is the elemental sense of being an experiencer of experiences. Awareness has an inherent subjectivity, a localization to a particular perspective (e.g., to my body, not yours). That localization is grounded in the body's engagement with the world. For example, when you turn your head to scan a room, what you see is specifically related to your own movements. The brain indexes across innumerable experiences to find the common feature: the experiencing of them in one particular body. In effect, subjectivity arises from the inherent distinction between *this* body and *that* world; in the broadest sense, subjectivity is generated not only in the brain but in the ongoing interactions the body has with the world (Thompson 2007).

Then the brain indexes across moments of subjectivity to create an apparent subject who—over the course of development, from infancy to adulthood—is elaborated and layered through the maturation of the brain, notably regions of the prefrontal cortex (Zelazo, Gao, and Todd 2007). But there is no subject *inherent* in subjectivity; in advanced meditation practices, one finds a bare awareness without a subject (Amaro 2003). Awareness requires subjectivity, but it does not require a subject.

In sum, from a neurological standpoint, the everyday feeling of being a unified self is an utter illusion: the apparently coherent and solid "I" is actually built from many subsystems and sub-subsystems over the course of development, with no fixed center, and the fundamental sense that there is a subject of experience is fabricated from myriad, disparate moments of subjectivity.

Self Is Just One Part of a Person

A *person* is a human body-mind as a whole, an autonomous and dynamic system that arises in dependence upon human culture and the natural world (Mackenzie 2009). You're a person and I'm a person. Persons have histories, values, and plans. They are morally culpable and reap the consequences of what they sow. The person goes on being as long as the body is alive and the brain is reasonably intact. But as we've seen, self-related mental contents have no special neurological status and are just part of the ongoing stream of mental activity. Whatever aspect of self that is momentarily active engages only a small fraction of the brain's many networks (Gusnard et al 2001; Legrand and Ruby 2009). Even those aspects of self that are stored in explicit and implicit memory take up only a portion of the brain's storehouse of information about the world, perceptual processing, skilled action, and more. The self is just one part of the whole person.

Further, most aspects of a person can buzz merrily along without an "I" directing them. For example, most of your thoughts arise without any deliberate creation. We all routinely engage in many mental and physical activities without "I" making them happen. In fact, often the less self the better, since that improves many kinds of task performance and emotional functioning (Koch and Tsuchiya 2006; Leary, Adams, and Tate 2006). Even when it seems like the self has made a conscious decision, that choice is often the result of unconscious factors (Galdi, Arcuri, and Gawronksi 2008; Libet 1999).

In particular, awareness does not need a self to operate. Aspects of self arise and disperse within awareness, but awareness persists as a field of consciousness independent of the vicissitudes of self. To experience this, be mindful of the first second or two of hearing or seeing something new. At first there is often just the barest perception crystallizing in awareness, with no sense of a being, an "I" who is perceiving it; then it's possible to observe a growing sense of self linked to the perception, particularly if it is personally significant. But it is directly apparent that *awareness can do its job without a subject.* We routinely presume that there is a subject of consciousness because consciousness entails subjectivity, as we saw above, and the brain indexes across moments of subjectivity to find an apparent subject. But subjectivity is just a way to structure experience; it's not an entity, a ghostly being looking out through your eyes. In fact, observing your own experience shows that the self—the apparent subject—often comes in after the fact. In many ways, the self is like someone running behind a parade that is already well under way, continually calling out: "See what I created!"

Self Keeps Changing

As different parts of self come forward and then give way to other parts, so do the momentary neural assemblies that enable them. If the energy flows of these assemblies could be seen as a play of light, an extraordinary show would move endlessly about your head. In the brain, *every manifestation of self is impermanent.* The self is continually constructed, deconstructed, and constructed again.

The self seems coherent and continuous because of how the brain forms conscious experience: imagine a thousand photographs overlaying each other, each one taking a few seconds to develop into a clear picture and then fade out. This composite construction of experience creates the illusion of integration and continuity, much like twenty-two static frames per second create the semblance of motion in a movie. Consequently, we experience "now" not as a thin sliver of time in which each snapshot of experience appears sharply and ends abruptly, but as a moving interval roughly 1–3 seconds long that blurs and fades at each end (Lutz et al. 2002; Thompson 2007).

It is not so much that we have a self, it's that we do self-ing. As Buckminster Fuller famously said, "I seem to be a verb."

Self Depends on Conditions

At any moment, the parts of self that are present depend on many factors, including genetic heritage, personal history, temperament, and situations. In particular, self depends a lot on the feeling tone of experience. When the feeling tone is neutral, the self tends to fade into the background. But as soon as something distinctly pleasant or unpleasant appears—for example, an interesting email or a physical pain—the self quickly mobilizes along the processing cascade that moves from feeling tone to craving, and from craving to clinging. The self organizes around strong desires. Which comes first: Do "I" form a desire? Or does desire form an "I?"

The self also depends greatly on social context. Walk along casually: often not much sense of self. But bump into an old acquaintance, and within seconds many parts of the self come online, such as memories of shared experiences—or wondering how you look.

Self never comes forward on its own. For starters, it developed over several million years, shaped by the twists and turns of evolution (Leary & Buttermore 2003). Then at any moment today, it arises through neural activities that depend on other bodily systems, and those systems depend on a network of supporting factors ranging from grocery stores to the seemingly arbitrary but remarkably provident physical constants of this universe, which enable the conditions for life such as stars, planets, and water. *The self has no inherent, unconditional, absolute existence* apart from the network of causes it arises from, in, and as (MacKenzie 2009).

Self Is Like a Unicorn

Self-related representations abound in the mind and thus in the brain. Those patterns of information and neural activity are certainly real. But that which they point to, explicitly or implicitly–a unified, enduring, independent "I" who is the essential owner of experiences and agent of actions–just doesn't exist. In the brain, self-related activities are distributed and compounded, not unified; they are variable and transient, not enduring; and they are dependent on changing conditions, including the interactions the body has with the world. Just because we have a sense of self does not mean that we are a self. The brain strings together heterogenous moments of self-ing and subjectivity into an illusion of homogenous coherence and continuity. The self is truly a fictional character. Sometimes it's useful to act as if it's real, as we'll see below. Play the role of the self when you need to. But try to keep remembering that who you are as a person–dynamically intertwined with the world–is more alive, interesting, capable, and remarkable than any self.

(AN APPARENT) SELF HAS ITS USES

An apparent self is good for some things. It is a convenient way to distinguish one person from another. It brings a sense of continuity to life's kaleidoscope of experiences, linked to each other by appearing to happen to a particular "me." It adds verve and commitment to relationships—"I love you" is a much more powerful statement than "There is love arising here."

A sense of self is present at birth in nascent form (Stern 2000), and children normally develop substantial self structures by age five; if they don't, their relationships are very impaired. Self-related processes are wired into the brain for good reasons. They helped our ancestors succeed in increasingly social hunter-gatherer bands in which interpersonal dynamics played a strong role in survival; reading the self in others and expressing one's own self skillfully were very useful in forming alliances, mating, and keeping children alive to pass on one's genes. The evolution of relationships fostered the evolution of self and vice versa; the benefits of self have thus been a factor in the evolution of the brain. Self has been stitched into human DNA by reproductive advantages slowly accumulating across a hundred thousand generations.

The point here isn't to defend or justify the self. But neither should we demean or suppress it. Just don't make self special—it's simply an arising mental pattern that's not categorically different from or better than any other mind-object. When you use the methods that follow, you're not resisting the self or making it a problem. You're just seeing through it and encouraging it to relax, to dissipate like morning fog clearing under the sun. And what's left behind? Open-hearted spaciousness, wisdom, values and virtues, and a soft sweet joy.

RELEASE IDENTIFICATION

One way the self grows is by equating itself to things—by identifying with them. Unfortunately, when you identify with something, you make its fate your own—and yet, everything in this world ultimately ends. So be mindful of how you identify with positions, objects, and people. A traditional inquiry is to ask questions like these: *Am I this hand? Am I this belief? Am I this sense of "I"? Am I this awareness?* Perhaps follow the question with an explicit answer, such as: *No, I am not this hand.*

Be especially watchful about identifying with the executive functions (e.g., monitoring, planning, choosing). Notice how often your brain just as successfully makes plans and choices *without* much "I" involved, such as while driving to work. Be mindful as well about identifying with awareness; allow awareness to arise without needing to identify with or direct it.

Regard "I," "me," "mine," and other forms of self as just more mind-objects—thoughts like any other. Remind yourself: *I am not thoughts. I am not these thoughts of "I."* Don't identify with the self! Don't use self words ("I," "me," "myself," and "mine") any more than necessary. Try to get through a specific period of time, such as an hour at work, without using them at all.

Let experiences flow through awareness without identifying with them. If this stance were verbalized, it would sound something like this: *Seeing is happening. There is sensation. Thoughts arise. A sense of self emerges.* Move, plan, feel, and talk with as little presumption of self as possible.

Extend this mindfulness to the mini-movies playing in the simulator of your mind. Notice how a presumption of self is embedded in most of these movies, even when the self is not an overt character. This embedding reinforces the self as neurons fire and wire together in your simulations. Instead, cultivate a general attitude, also reaching into the mini-movies, that events can be perceived from the perspective of a particular body-mind without there needing to be an "I" to do the perceiving.

GENEROSITY

Self also grows through possessiveness. Self is like a knotted fist: when you open the hand to give, there's no more fist—no more self.

You can give so much in this life, and that offers you many opportunities to release the self. For example, you can give time, helpfulness, donations, restraint, patience, noncontention, and forgiveness. Any path of service—including raising a family, caring for others, and many kinds of work—incorporates generosity.

Envy—and its close cousin, jealousy—is a major impediment to generosity. So notice the suffering in envy, how it is an affliction upon *you*. Envy actually activates some of the same neural networks involved with physical pain (Takahashi et al. 2009). In a compassionate and kind way, remind yourself that you will be all right even if other people have fame, money, or a great partner—and you don't. To free yourself from the clutches of envy, send compassion and loving-kindness to people you envy. Once, on a meditation retreat, I was thinking enviously about some people and found a surprising peace in this wish toward them: *May you have all the success that I lack.*

Also, observe perceptions, thoughts, emotions, and other mind-objects, and inquire: *Does this have an owner?* Then observe the truth of things: *This has no owner.* It's fruitless to try to possess the mind; no one owns it.

HEALTHY HUMILITY

Perhaps most of all, self grows through self-importance; its antidote is healthy humility. Being humble means being natural and unassuming, *not* being a doormat, ashamed, or inferior. It just means you're not setting your self above others. Humility feels peaceful. You don't have to work at impressing people, and no one is at odds with you for being pretentious or judgmental.

Be Good to Yourself

Paradoxically, it supports humility to take good care of yourself, since self networks in your brain activate when you feel threatened or unsupported. To reduce this activation, make sure your fundamental needs are well cared for. For example, we all need to feel cherished. Empathy, praise, and love from others—especially in childhood—are internalized in neural networks that support feelings of confidence and worth. But if you receive these in short supply over the years, you're likely to end up with a hole in your heart.

The self gets very busy around that hole! Trying to put a lid on the hole through cockiness or to get a momentary "fix" through clinginess. Besides being annoying to others—leading you to receive less empathy, praise, and love than ever—these strategies are pointless, since they don't address the fundamental issue.

Instead, fill the hole in your heart by taking in the good (see chapter 4), one brick at a time. When I was younger, the hole in my heart looked about as big as the excavation for a skyscraper. When I realized that it should and *could* get filled, I deliberately looked for evidence of my worth, such as the love and respect of others, and my good qualities and accomplishments. Then I'd take a few seconds to soak in the experience. After several weeks and lots of bricks, I started to feel different; within a few months, there was a significantly greater sense of personal worth. Now, many years and thousands of bricks later, that hole in my heart is pretty full.

No matter how big your own hole is, each day hands you at least a few bricks for it. Pay attention to good things about yourself and the caring and acknowledgement of others—and then take them in. No single brick will eliminate that hole. But if you keep at it, day by day, brick by brick, you'll truly fill it up.

Like many practices, being good to yourself is a kind of raft to get you across the river of suffering—to use a metaphor from the Buddha. When you get to the other side, you'll no longer need the raft. You'll have built up your internal resources to the point that you won't have to consciously look for evidence of your worth anymore.

Relax About What Others Think

We evolved to care greatly about our reputation, since reputation affected whether others in the band would help or hurt an individual's chances of survival (Bowles 2006). It is wholly human to wish to be respected and even cherished, and to seek that for yourself. But getting caught up in what others think is a different matter. As Shantideva said (1999, p.113):

Why should I be pleased when people praise me?
Others there will be who scorn and criticize.
And why despondent when I'm blamed,
Since there'll be others who think well of me?

Consider how much time you spend thinking—in even the subtlest way, in the back of the simulator—about what others think of you. Be mindful of doing things to get admiration and praise. Try to focus instead on just doing the best you can. Think about virtue, benevolence, and wisdom: if you sincerely keep trying to come from these, that's about all you can do. And it's a lot!

You Don't Need to Be Special

Believing that you need to be special in order to deserve love and support sets a really high bar that takes much effort and strain to clear—day after day after day. And it sets you up for self-criticism and feelings of inadequacy and worthlessness if you don't get the recognition you crave. Instead, try wishing yourself well in these ways: *May I be loved without being special. May I contribute without being special.*

Consider renouncing specialness—including being important and admired. Renunciation is the antithesis of clinging, and thus a radical path to happiness. Say phrases like these in your mind, and notice what they feel like: *I give up being important. I renounce seeking approval.* Feel the peace in this surrender.

Love the *person* you are, much as you would care about any person dear to you. But don't love the *self* or any other mere mind-object.

JOINED WITH THE WORLD

The sense of self grows when you separate from the world. Therefore, deepening the sense of connection with the world will reduce the sense of self.

To live, to have a metabolism, your body must be joined with the world through continuing exchanges of energy and matter. Similarly, your brain isn't fundamentally separate from the rest of the body that feeds and protects it. Therefore, in a deep sense your brain is joined with the world (Thompson and Varela 2001). And as we've seen many times, the mind and the brain form an integrated system. Consequently, your mind and the world are intimately joined together.

You can help this recognition deepen in a variety of ways:

- Reflect on the flows of food, water, and sunlight that sustain your body. See yourself as an animal like any other in your dependence on the natural world. Spend time in nature.

- Pay attention to the aspect of *space* in your environments, such as the empty volume of air in your living room, or the space through which cars move on your way to work. Doing this naturally draws awareness to things as a whole.

- Think bigger and wider. For example, when you buy gasoline, consider the great network of causes that help produce the apparent self—driving its car, perhaps feeling stressed or preoccupied—including the gas station, global economics, and ultimately, ancient plankton and algae crushed under the earth into oil. See how those causes depend on an even vaster network that includes the solar system, our galaxy, other galaxies, and the physical processes of the material realm. Try to feel the living truth that you arise and abide in dependence upon the whole universe. The Milky Way is here because of the local group of galaxies; the sun is here because of the Milky Way; and you're here because of the sun—so in some ways you're here because of galaxies millions of light years away.

- If you can, go all the way out to the ultimate frame: the allness, the totality that is everything. For example, the world you see at hand, including your body and mind within it, is always just one whole thing. At any moment, you can notice this one allness. Its parts change, endlessly. They unravel, decay, and disperse, every single one of them. Therefore, no part can ever be a reliable, enduring source of true happiness—including the self. But the allness as allness never changes. The whole remains reliably whole. The whole never clings and suffers. Ignorance contracts from the totality into the self. Wisdom reverses that process, emptying the self out into allness.

It's a wonderful paradox that as individual things—such as the self—feel increasingly groundless and unreliable, the totality of everything feels increasingly safe and comforting. As the sense of groundlessness grows, each apparently individual thing seems a bit like a cloud that you'll fall through if you try to stand on it. At first this is pretty unnerving. But then you realize that the sky itself— the totality—is holding you up. You are walking on the sky *because you're sky*. It has always been that way. You and every one else have been sky all along.

JOINED WITH LIFE

One time a friend of mine went on a meditation retreat in a forest monastery in Burma. He took vows, including not to intentionally kill any living being. After a couple of weeks, his meditation was not going very well. He also began to wonder about the latrine near his hut. It was a pit toilet, and after using it, he was supposed to clean the area around the hole with water, but there were usually ants nearby which were washed away. He asked the abbot if this was all right. "No," the abbot said simply, "that's not your vow." My friend took the abbot's comment seriously, and started cleaning the toilet much more carefully. And, perhaps not coincidentally, his meditation deepened dramatically.

How often do we place our convenience ahead of the life of another being, even an ant on a toilet? It's not deliberately cruel, but it is self-centered. Look the creature in the eye—the mosquito, the mouse—and know that it wants to live, just like you do. How would it feel to be killed for someone's *convenience*?

If you want, take on the practice of never killing for your own convenience. This will draw you into feeling more kinship with all life, you as a creature in harmony with other beings. You'll be treating the world as an extension of yourself: not harming yourself entails not harming the world.

Similarly, kindness to the world is kindness to yourself. As the self starts to relax and fall away, you can really wonder how to live. Once on a retreat, I experienced such a strong sense of everything as a whole that I began to despair at the utter unimportance of my tiny part of it. My life could not possibly matter. After hardly sleeping, I sat outside the dining hall before breakfast, near a little creek, with a doe and her fawn grazing under the trees close by. I began to feel very deeply that each living thing has its nature and its place in the whole. The doe licked her fawn, nuzzling and nibbling it. She clearly belonged where she was, eventually to die and disperse but meanwhile thriving and contributing in her own way. Insects and birds rustled in the fallen leaves as well: all moving about, each one creating benefits for the whole in some way.

Just as each of those animals had its place and its contributions, I had my own. Not one of us was important. But it was all right to be in my place and thrive there. It was all right to relax and be the whole. To be the whole expressed as a part, to be a part expressing the whole.

Sometime later a gray squirrel and I watched each other from just a few feet apart. It was natural to wish that squirrel well, that it find acorns and dodge owls. (And, in the complexity of the forest, to wish the owl well too, that it find a squirrel to ease its hunger.) We looked at each other for a strangely long time, and I truly wished the best for that squirrel. Then another thing came clear: I was an organism, too, just like the squirrel. It was all right to wish myself well just like any other living being.

It is all right to wish yourself well, just like wishing the best for any living being. It is all right to do well according to your nature, with a human brain, going as far as you can in this life down the path of happiness, love, and wisdom.

What remains when self disperses, even temporarily? The wholehearted movement to contribute, and the wish to thrive and prosper as one human animal among six billion. To be healthy and strong and live many more years. To be caring and kind. To awaken, abiding as radiant, spacious, loving consciousness. To feel protected and supported. To be happy and comfortable, serene and fulfilled. To live and love in peace.

---

chapter 13: KEY POINTS

🪷 It's ironic and poignant that the "I" makes you suffer in many ways. When you take things personally, identify with or try to possess things that inevitably end, or separate yourself from all things, you suffer. But when you relax the sense of self and flow with life, you feel happy and satisfied.

🪷 When you take the body for a walk—or do just about anything—without much sense of self, you discover some interesting things: the self usually feels a little contracted and tense, it is often unnecessary, and it continually changes. The self gets especially activated in response to opportunities and threats; desires often form an "I" before an "I" forms desires.

🪷 Thoughts, feelings, images, and such exist as patterns of information based on patterns of neural structure and activity. In the same way, representations of the self and the sense of being a self exist as patterns in the mind and brain. The question is not whether those patterns exist. The key questions are: What is their *nature*? And does that which they point to—a unified, ongoing owner of experiences and agent of actions—truly exist?

💮 The many aspects of self are based on numerous neural networks. These networks perform many functions unrelated to the self, and representations of self within them don't appear to have any neurologically special status.

💮 The self is just part of the person. Most thoughts, plans, and actions don't need a self to direct them. Self-related neural networks comprise only a small part of the brain, and an even smaller part of the nervous system.

💮 The self keeps changing; in the brain, every manifestation of the self is impermanent. Just as the individual frames in a movie create the illusion of motion, the overlapping neural assemblies that flow together and then disperse create the illusion of a coherent and continuous self.

💮 The self arises and changes depending on various conditions, notably pleasant and unpleasant feeling tones. It also depends on relationships—including with the wider world. The most fundamental basis for the sense of "I"—the subjectivity inherent in awareness—emerges in the relationship between the body and the world. The self has no independent existence whatsoever.

💮 Self-related mental activity, including the sense of being the subject of experience, refers to a unified, enduring, independent "I" who is the essential owner of experiences and agent of actions—but such a one does not exist. The self is a collection of real representations of an unreal being—like a story about a unicorn.

✤ The apparent self is useful for relationships and for a healthy sense of psychological coherence over time. Humans have a sense of self because it served vital survival functions during our evolution. It is pointless to be averse to the self, since aversion intensifies the self. The point is to see through the self and let it relax and disperse.

✤ The self grows through identification, possession, pride, and separation from the world and life. We explored many ways to disengage from these and, instead, center increasingly in openhearted spaciousness, goodwill toward one's own thriving, and contented peaceful relationships with other beings.

Appendix

Nutritional Neurochemistry

—Jan Hanson, L.Ac.

The previous chapters have explored how to influence the brain through mental interventions. This appendix will summarize ways to support brain function through the *physical* intervention of skillful nutrition. Of course, none of these suggestions are a substitute for professional care, nor are they aimed at treating any medical condition.

As an acupuncturist who has focused on clinical nutrition for many years—and needed to apply some of its lessons to herself!—I've repeatedly seen that small, thoughtful, sensible changes in what you put into your mouth each day can gradually produce significant benefits. And sometimes these steps—such as taking nutrients you've needed for a long time—can lead to rapid improvements in your well-being.

DIET BASICS

Help your brain by eating well every day, minimizing your sugar intake, and avoiding food allergens.

Eat Well Every Day

Take in a wide variety of rich nutrients. More than anything, this means eating lots of protein and vegetables. Eat protein at every meal; aim for a portion roughly the size of your palm. Eat at least three cups of vegetables a day—more is better! Ideally, half of your plate at each meal will be covered by vegetables of all kinds and colors. Fruits also provide important nutrition; berries in particular are known to be good for your brain (Galli et al. 2006; Joseph et al. 2003).

Minimize Sugar

Keep your sugar under control. High blood sugar wears on the hippocampus (Wu et al. 2008). Impaired glucose tolerance—a sign of eating too much sugar—is linked to relative cognitive impairment in older adults (Messier and Gagnon 2000). The best way to minimize sugar is to avoid refined sugar altogether (especially in sugary drinks) as well as foods made from refined flour (e.g., bread, noodles, cookies).

Avoid Food Allergens

Eating foods to which you are sensitive will cause an allergic and inflammatory reaction throughout your body, not just in your digestive system. Chronic inflammation, even if relatively mild, is an enemy of the brain. For example, gluten sensitivities have been linked to a variety of neurological disorders (Hadjivassiliou, Gunwale, and Davies-Jones 2002; Hadjivassiliou et al. 1996). Even without a known sensitivity, increased consumption of milk correlates with an increased risk of Parkinson's disease (Park et al. 2005).

The most common food allergens are products made from cow milk, gluten grains (wheat, oats, rye, barley, spelt, and kamut), and soy. Food allergies can be formally identified through blood tests done by a medical lab. Informally, try eliminating foods you suspect may be problematic for a week or two, and then notice if you feel better, think more clearly, digest more easily, and have more energy.

FUNDAMENTAL SUPPLEMENTS FOR YOUR BRAIN

Vitamins and minerals are cofactors in thousands of metabolic processes. They support every aspect of your health, including the functioning of your brain and mind (Kaplan et al. 2007). So it's important to get enough of these to take care of all of your needs. Unless you spend a lot of time acquiring and preparing fresh foods, you probably aren't getting optimal quantities of vitamins and minerals through your diet alone. Therefore, it makes sense to supplement them prudently.

Take a High Potency Multivitamin/ Multimineral Supplement

A good multivitamin/multimineral supplement is your insurance policy; it will help you get a wide variety of essential nutrients. While all nutrients are important, put a special focus on the B vitamins, which are particularly vital for brain health. Vitamins B-12, B-6, and folic acid all help a biochemical process called *methylation*, which plays a crucial role in the production of many neurotransmitters. When you are deficient in these B vitamins, your homocysteine (an amino acid) level may become elevated. Low B vitamins and high homocysteine are risk factors for cognitive decline and dementia in older people (Clarke et al. 2007; Vogiatzoglou et al. 2008). Low folic acid is also a risk factor for depression; supplementing it can relieve depressive symptoms (A. Miller 2008).

Your multivitamin supplement should contain 10–25 times the daily value of all of the B vitamins, and 800 mcg or more of folic acid (Marz 1999). It should have most minerals at 100 percent or more of the daily value. To consume these levels, you may need to augment your general multi with additional supplements.

Take Omega-3 Fatty Acids

The omega-3 fatty acids found in fish oil—docosahexaenoic acid (DHA) and eicosapentaenoic acid (EPA)—provide many benefits to your brain; these include promotion of neuronal growth, mood elevation, and slowing of dementia (Ma et al. 2007; Puri 2006; Singh 2005; Su et al. 2003). DHA is the predominant structural fatty acid in the central nervous system, and its availability is crucial for brain development. EPA is an important anti-inflammatory molecule.

Take enough fish oil to consume at least 500 milligrams of DHA daily, and about the same amount of EPA (Hyman 2009). Look for a high-quality source—one that is molecularly distilled; most people prefer capsules to taking fish oil directly.

Or, if you're a vegetarian, take a full tablespoon of flax seed oil daily (perhaps in salad dressing, but don't cook with it). Although flax seed oil converts into DHA and EPA, in most people this conversion is inefficient and incomplete. Consequently, add 500 mg of DHA from algae to your flax seed oil.

Take Vitamin E as Gamma-Tocopherol

Vitamin E is the main antioxidant in the cellular membranes within your brain (Kidd 2005). The most common form of vitamin E consumed through the diet is gamma-tocopherol, which makes up 70 percent of total vitamin-E intake.

Unfortunately, nutritional supplements usually contain alpha-tocopherol, another form of vitamin E. Alpha-tocopherol seems to be less beneficial than gamma-tocopherol, and it dilutes the gamma-tocopherol you naturally get from your diet. This may be one reason why studies of vitamin-E supplementation have produced mixed results. However, one study found that older people who consumed higher levels of vitamin E—primarily in the form of gamma-tocopherol—had less risk of developing Alzheimer's disease and slower rates of cognitive decline (Morris et al. 2005).

More research is needed, but in the meantime it seems reasonable to take a supplement of vitamin E that contains a mixture of the tocopherols, with gamma-tocopherol in the majority. Take a supplement that has about 400 IU of vitamin E (Marz 1999), at least half of which is gamma-tocopherol (Hyman 2009).

NUTRITIONAL SUPPORT FOR NEUROTRANSMITTERS

You can affect the levels of your neurotransmitters through targeted nutritional interventions. But be careful about it. Start with the smallest dosage and respect your own nature; individual responses vary significantly. Try one supplement at a time, making sure you feel good with the first one before adding another. Discontinue a supplement immediately if you experience any negative side effects. Don't use these supplements if you are taking an antidepressant or other psychotropic medication unless your doctor tells you otherwise.

Serotonin

Serotonin supports mood, digestion, and sleep. It's made from the amino acid tryptophan in essentially two steps: tryptophan is converted into 5-hydroxytryptophan (5-HTP), which is then turned into serotonin. Nutritional cofactors are required for these conversions, notably iron and vitamin B-6 (as pyridoxal-5-phosphate or P5P) (Murray et al. 2000). Therefore, the following nutrients can help with serotonin production; you can use them in combination, if you wish.

IRON

If you feel fatigued or depressed, talk to your physician about the possibility that your iron level is low. Additionally, many menstruating women have low iron levels. A blood test is required to know if you're anemic; if you are, you can take an iron supplement, and the proper dosage will depend on your lab results.

VITAMIN B-6

Vitamin B-6 is a co-factor in dozens—perhaps hundreds—of important metabolic processes, including the production of several neurotransmitters (e.g., serotonin). Take 50 mg of vitamin B-6 (as P5P) on an empty stomach in the morning.

5-HYDROXYTRYPTOPHAN AND TRYPTOPHAN

Take 50–200 mg of 5-HTP in the morning or 500–1,500 mg of tryptophan before bed (Hyman 2009; Marz 1999). If you are primarily focused on lifting your mood, take 5-HTP in the morning. It is unlikely to make you sleepy, and it is the most direct route to serotonin. If insomnia is an issue, start with tryptophan just before bed, since it's more likely to enhance your sleep.

Norepinephrine and Dopamine

Norepinephrine and dopamine are excitatory neurotransmitters that support energy, mood, and attention. The process of creating these neurotransmitters begins with the amino acid L-phenylalanine.

This is converted into L-tyrosine, which gets made into dopamine; in turn, dopamine is transformed further into norepinephrine (Murray et al. 2000).

As with serotonin, iron and vitamin B-6 (as P5P) are necessary cofactors for these conversions. Therefore, supplementing these can increase norepinephrine and dopamine. Because optimizing serotonin before enhancing dopamine and norepinephrine often feels better than the reverse, start with the nutrients that build serotonin. Take these for two weeks or so before considering phenylalanine or tyrosine.

For some people, phenylalanine and tyrosine supplements feel too stimulating. If you feel nervous or hyper after taking them, stop. To be cautious, start with a low dose of 500 mg or less, taken on an empty stomach in the morning. If you like the effects, you can increase the dose up to 1,500 mg per day (Hyman 2009). Of these two amino acids, tyrosine is the most direct route to making norepinephrine and dopamine; consequently, it's used more often, though some people prefer L-phenylalanine. Either one is fine.

Acetylcholine

Acetylcholine supports memory and attention. To build this neurotransmitter, you need rich sources of choline in your diet, such as egg yolks (possibly the best source), beef, liver, or dairy fats. Also consider the following supplements; if you decide to try supplementation, introduce one supplement at a time. Find the individual supplement or combination (potentially including all three) that feels best for you.

PHOSPHATIDYLSERINE

Phosphatidylserine (PS) is the major acidic phospholipid in the brain, and a key component of the brain's cellular membranes. Phospholipids play an important role in communication between brain cells. PS supports acetylcholine (Pedata et al. 1985), and seems to aid memory. You can take 100–300 mg per day (Hyman 2009).

ACETYL-L-CARNITINE

Acetyl-L-carnitine seems to help with memory problems and Alzheimer's disease, perhaps through its effect on acetylcholine pathways (Spagnoli et al. 1991). Try 500–1,000 mg per day on an empty stomach in the morning (Hyman 2009). If you're sensitive to stimulating nutrients, you may want to try this one last.

HUPERZINE-A

Extracted from Chinese club moss, huperzine-A slows the metabolic breakdown of acetylcholine and thus appears to enhance memory and attention (Cheng, Ren, and Xi 1996; Sun et al. 1999). Try 50–200 mcg per day (Hyman 2009).

CHANGE FROM THE GROUND FLOOR ON UP

Your brain is made from trillions of molecules, most of which have come from what you've put in your mouth at one time or another. Through making small changes in your diet and supplements, you can gradually change the components of your brain, from the molecular ground floor on up. As the physical substrate of your brain improves, you're likely to experience greater physical and mental well-being, and your psychological and spiritual practices—including the methods described in this book—will become even more fruitful.

References

Allman, J., A. Hakeem, J. Erwin, E. Nimchinsy, and P. Hop. 2001. The anterior cingulate cortex: The evolution of an interface between emotion and cognition. *Annals of the New York Academy of Sciences*, 935:107–117.

Amaro. 2003. *Small Boat, Great Mountain: Theravadan Reflections on the Natural Great Perfection*. Redwood Valley, CA: Abhayagiri Buddhist Monastery.

Aron, A., H. Fisher, D. Mashek, G. Strong, H. Li, and L. Brown. 2005. Reward, motivation, and emotion systems associated with early-stage intense romantic love. *Journal of Neurophysiology* 94:327–337.

Aspinwall, L. G. and S. E. Taylor. 1997. A stitch in time: Self-regulation and proactive coping. *Psychological Bulletin* 121:417–436.

Atmanspacher, H. and P. Graben. 2007. Contextual emergence of mental states from neurodynamics. *Chaos and Complexity Letters* 2:151–168.

Baars, B. J. 1997. In the theatre of consciousness: Global workspace theory, a rigorous scientific theory of consciousness. *Journal of Consciousness Studies* 4:292.

Balter, M. 2007. Brain evolution studies go micro. *Science* 315:1208–1211.

Bard, K. A. 2006. Are humans the only primates that cry? *Scientific American Mind* 17:83.

Bateson, M., D. Nettle, and G. Robert. 2006. Cues of being watched enhance cooperation in a real-world setting. *Biology Letters* 2:412–414.

Baumeister, R., E. Bratlavsky, C. Finkenauer, and K. Vohs. 2001. Bad is stronger than good. *Review of General Psychology* 5:323–370.

Begley, S. 2007. *Train Your Mind, Change Your Brain: How a New Science Reveals Our Extraordinary Potential to Transform Ourselves.* New York: Ballantine Books.

Benson, H. 2000. *The Relaxation Response.* New York: Harper Paperbacks.

Bowles, S. 2006. Group competition, reproductive leveling, and the evolution of human altruism. *Science* 314:1569–1572.

———. 2009. Did warfare among ancestral hunter-gatherers affect the evolution of human social behaviors? *Science* 324:1293-1298.

Brahm, A. 2006. *Mindfulness, Bliss, and Beyond: A Meditator's Handbook.* Boston: Wisdom Publications.

Braver, T. and J. Cohen. 2000. On the control of control: The role of dopamine in regulating prefrontal function and working memory. In *Control of Cognitive Processes: Attention and Performance XVIII*, edited by S. Monsel and J. Driver. Cambridge, MA: MIT Press.

Braver, T., D. Barch, and J. Cohen. 2002. The role of prefrontal cortex in normal and disordered cognitive control: A cognitive neuroscience perspective. In *Principles of Frontal Lobe Function*, edited by D. T. Stuss and R. T. Knight. New York: Oxford University Press.

Brehony, K. A. 2001. *After the Darkest Hour: How Suffering Begins the Journey to Wisdom.* New York: Macmillan.

Brickman, P., D. Coates, and R. Janoff-Bulman. 1978. Lottery winners or accident victims: Is happiness relative? *Journal of Personality and Social Psychology* 36:917–927.

Buschman, T. and E. Miller. 2007. Top-down versus bottom-up control of attention in the prefrontal and posterior parietal cortices. *Science* 315:1860–1862.

Carter, O. L., D. E. Presti, C. Callistemon, Y. Ungerer, G. B. Liu, and J. D. Pettigrew. 2005. Meditation alters perceptual rivalry in Tebetan Buddhist monks. *Current Biology* 15:412–413.

Cheney, D. L. and R. M. Seyfarth. 2008. *Baboon Metaphysics: The Evolution of a Social Mind*. Chicago: University of Chicago Press.

Cheng, D. H., H. T. Ren, and C. Xi. 1996. Huperzine A, a novel promising acetylcholinesterase inhibitor. *NeuroReport* 8:97–101.

Choi, J. and S. Bowles. 2007. The coevolution of parochial altruism and war. *Science* 318:636–640.

Clarke, R., J. Birks, E. Nexo, P. M. Ueland, J. Schneede, J. Scott, A. Molloy, and J. G. Evans. 2007. Low vitamin B-12 status and risk of cognitive decline in older adults. *American Journal of Clinical Nutrition* 86:1384–1391.

Cohen, J., G. Aston-Jones, and M. Gilzenrat. 2005. A systems-level perspective on attention and cognitive control. In *Cognitive Neuroscience of Attention*, edited by M. Posner. New York: Guilford Press.

Coward, F. 2008. Standing on the shoulders of giants. *Science* 319:1493–1495.

Cunningham, W. and P. D. Zelazo. 2007. Attitudes and evaluations: A social cognitive neuroscience perspective. *Trends in Cognitive Sciences* 11:97–104.

D'Amasio, A. 2000. *The Feeling of What Happens: Body and Emotion in the Making of Consciousness*. Orlando, FL: Harvest Books.

Davidson, R. J. 2004. Well-being and affective style: Neural substrates and biobehavioural correlates. *Philosophical Transactions of the Royal Society* 359:1395–1411.

Davidson, R. J., J. Kabat-Zinn, J. Schumacher, M. Rosenkranz, D. Muller, S. F. Santorelli, F. Urbanowski, A. Harrington, K. Bonus, and J. F. Sheridan. 2003. Alterations in brain and immune function produced by mindfulness meditation. *Psychosomatic Medicine* 65:564–570.

Dehaene, S., C. Sergent, and J. Changeux. 2003. A neuronal network model linking subjective reports and objective physiological data during conscious perception. *Proceedings of the National Academy of Sciences* 100:8520–8525.

de Quervain, D. U. Fischbacher, V. Treyer, M. Schellhammer, U. Schnyder, A. Buck, and E. Fehr. 2004. The neural basis of altruistic punishment. *Science* 305:1254–1258.

de Waal, F. 2006. *Primates and Philosophers: How Morality Evolved.* Princeton, NJ: Princeton University Press.

Dobzhansky, T. 1973. Nothing in biology makes sense except in the light of evolution. *American Biology Teacher* 35:125–129.

Dunbar, R. I. M. and S. Shultz. 2007. Evolution in the social brain. *Science* 317:1344–1347.

Dunn, E. W., L. B. Aknin, and M. Norton. 2008. Spending money on others promotes happiness. *Science* 319:1687–1688.

Dusek, J. A., H. H. Out, A. L. Wohlhueter, M. Bhasin, L. F. Zerbini, M. G. Joseph, H. Benson, and T. A. Libermann. 2008. Genomic counter-stress changes induced by the relaxation response. *PLoS ONE* 3:e2576.

Efferson, C., R. Lalive, and E. Feh. 2008. The coevolution of cultural groups and ingroup favoritism. *Science* 321:1844–1849.

Eisenberger, N. I., and M. D. Lieberman. 2004. Why rejection hurts: A common neural alarm system for physical and social pain. *Trends in Cognitive Science* 8:294–300.

Ekman, P. 2007. *Emotions Revealed: Recognizing Faces and Feelings to Improve Communication and Emotional Life,* 2nd ed. New York: Holt and Company LLC.

Engel, A. K., P. Fries, and W. Singer. 2001. Dynamic predictions: Oscillations and synchrony in top-down processing. *Nature Reviews Neuroscience* 2:704–716.

Farb, N. A. S., Z. V. Segal, H. Mayberg, J. Bean, D. McKeon, Z. Fatima, and A. Anderson. Attending to the present: Mindfulness meditation reveals distinct neural modes of self-reference. *Social Cognitive and Affective Neuroscience* 2:313–322.

Fisher, H. E., A. Aron, and L. Brown. 2006. Romantic love: A mammalian brain system for mate choice. *Philosophical Transactions of the Royal Society* 361:2173–2186.

Fiske, S. T. 2002. What we know about bias and intergroup conflict, the problem of the century. *Current Directions in Psychological Science* 11:123–128.

Frederickson, B. L. 2000. Cultivating positive emotions to optimize health and well-being. *Prevention and Treatment* Vol. 3: Article 0001a, posted online March 7, 2000.

———. 2001. The role of positive emotions in positive psychology. *American Psychologist* 56:218–226.

Frederickson, B. L. and R. Levenson. 1998. Positive emotions speed recovery from the cardiovascular sequelae of negative emotions. *Psychology Press* 12:191–220.

Frederickson, B. L., R. Mancuso, C. Branigan, and M. Tugade. 2000. The undoing effect of positive emotions. *Motivation and Emotion* 24:237–258.

Fronsdal, G, trans. 2006. *The Dhammapada: A New Translation of the Buddhist Classic with Annotations.* Boston: Shambhala.

Galdi, S., L. Arcuri, and B. Gawronski. 2008. Automatic mental associations predict future choices of undecided decision makers. *Science* 321:1100–1102.

Gallagher, S. 2000. Philosophical conceptions of the self: Implications for cognitive science. *Trends in Cognitive Sciences* 4:14–21.

Gallagher, H. and C. Frith. 2003. Functional imaging of "theory of mind." *Trends in Cognitive Sciences* 7:77–83.

Galli, R. L., D. F. Bielinski, A. Szprengiel, B. Shukitt-Hale, and J. A. Joseph. 2006. Blueberry supplemented diet reverses age-related decline in hippocampal HSP70 neuroprotection. *Neurobiology of Aging* 27:344–350.

Gaskin, S. 2005. *Monday Night Class.* Summertown, TN: Book Publishing Company.

Gibbons, A. 2008. The birth of childhood. *Science* 322:1040–1043.

Gillihan, S., and M. Farah. 2005. Is self special? A critical review of evidence from experimental psychology and cognitive neuroscience. *Psychological Bulletin* 131:76–97.

Gottman, J. 1995. *Why Marriages Succeed or Fail: And How You Can Make Yours Last.* New York: Simon and Schuster.

Gould, E., P. Tanapat, N. B. Hastings, T. Shors. 1999. Neurogenesis in adulthood: A possible role in learning. *Trends in Cognitive Sciences* 3:186–192.

Gross, J. J. and O. P. John. 2003. Individual differences in two emotion regulation processes: Implications for affect, relationships, and well-being. *Journal of Personality and Social Psychology* 85:348–362.

Guastella, A. J., P. U. B. Mitchell, and M. R. Dads. 2008. Oxytocin increases gaze to the eye region of human faces. *Biological Psychiatry* 305:3–5.

Gusnard, D. A., E. Abuja, G. I. Schulman, and M. E. Raichle. 2001. Medial prefrontal cortex and self-referential mental activity: Relation to a default mode of brain function. *Proceedings of the National Academy of Sciences* 98:4259–4264.

Hadjivassiliou, M., A. Gibson, G. A. B. Davies-Jones, A. J. Lobo, T. J. Stephenson, and A. Milford-Ward. 1996. Does cryptic gluten sensitivity play a part in neurological illness? *Lancet* 347:369–371.

Hadjivassiliou, M., R. A. Gunwale, and G. A. B. Davies-Jones. 2002. Gluten sensitivity as a neurological illness. *Journal of Neurology, Neurosurgery and Psychiatry* 72:560–563.

Haidt, J. 2007. The new synthesis in moral psychology. *Science* 316:998–1002.

Han, S., and G. Northoff. 2008. Culture-sensitive neural substrates of human cognition: A transcultural neuroimaging approach. *Nature Reviews Neuroscience* 9: 646–654.

Hanson, R., J. Hanson, and R. Pollycove. 2002. *Mother Nurture: A Mother's Guide to Health in Body, Mind, and Intimate Relationships.* New York: Penguin.

Harbaugh, W. T., U. Mayr, and D. R. Burghart. 2007. Neural responses to taxation and voluntary giving reveal motives for charitable donations. *Science* 316:1622–1625.

Hariri, A. R., S. Y. Bookheimer, and J. C. Mazziotta. 2000. Modulating emotional responses: Effects of a neocortical network on the limbic system. *NeuroReport* 11:43–48.

Hebb, D. O. 1949. *The organization of behavior.* New York: Wiley.

Herrmann, E., J. Call, H. Hernández-Lloreda, B. Hare, and M. Tomasello. 2007. Humans have evolved specialized skills of social cognition: The cultural intelligence hypothesis. *Science* 317:1358–1366.

Hölzel, B. K., U. Ott, T. Gard, H. Hempel, M. Weygandt, K. Morgen, and D. Vaitl. 2008. Investigation of mindfulness meditation practitioners with voxel-based morphometry. *Social Cognitive and Affective Neuroscience* 3:55–61.

Hyman, M. 2009. *The UltraMind Solution.* New York: Scribner.

Jankowiak, W., and E. Fischer. 1992. Romantic love: A cross-cultural perspective. *Ethnology* 31:149–155.

Jha, A. P., J. Krompinger, and M. J. Baime. 2007. Mindfulness training modifies subsystems of attention. *Cognitive, Affective, Behavioral Neuroscience* 7:109–119.

Jiang, Y., and S. He. 2006. Cortical responses to invisible faces: Dissociating subsystems for facial-information processing. *Current Biology* 16:2023–2029.

Joseph, J. A., N. A. Denisova, G. Arendash, M. Gordon, D. Diamond, B. Shukitt-Hale, and D. Morgan. 2003. Blueberry supplementation enhances signaling and prevents behavioral deficits in an Alzheimer disease model. *Nutritional Neuroscience* 6(3):153–162.

Judson, O. 2007. The selfless gene. *Atlantic,* October, 90–97.

Kaplan, B. J., S. G. Crawford, C. J. Field, and J. S. A. Simpson. 2007. Vitamins, minerals, and mood. *Psychological Bulletin* 133:747–760.

Keeley, L. H. 1997. *War Before Civilization: The Myth of the Peaceful Savage.* New York: Oxford University Press.

Kidd, P. 2005. Neurodegeneration from mitochondrial insufficiency: Nutrients, stem cells, growth factors, and prospects for brain rebuilding using integrative management. *Alternative Medicine Review* 10:268–293.

Knoch, D., A. Pascual-Leone, K. Meyer, V. Treyer, and E. Fehr. 2006. Diminishing reciprocal fairness by disrupting the right prefrontal cortex. *Science* 314:829–832.

Koch, C., and N. Tsuchiya. 2006. Attention and consciousness: Two distinct brain processes. *Trends in Cognitive Sciences* 11:16–22.

Kocsis, B. and R. P. Vertes. 1994. Characterization of neurons of the supramammillary nucleus and mammillary body that discharge rhythmically with the hippocampal theta rhythm in the rat. *Journal of Neuroscience* 14:7040–7052.

Kornfield, J. 1996. *Teachings of the Buddha.* Boston: Shambhala.

Kosfeld, M., M. Heinrichs, P. Zak, U. Fischbacher, and E. Fehr. 2005. Oxytocin increases trust in humans. *Nature* 435:673–676.

Kristal-Boneh, E., M. Raifel, P. Froom, and J. Ribak. 1995. Heart rate variability in health and disease. *Scandinavian Journal of Work, Environment, and Health* 21:85–95.

Lammert, E. 2008. Brain wnts for blood vessels. *Science* 322:1195–1196.

Lazar, S., C. Kerr, R. Wasserman, J. Gray, D. Greve, M. Treadway, M. McGarvey, B. Quinn, J. Dusek, H. Benson, S. Rauch, C. Moore, and B. Fischl. 2005. Meditation experience is associated with increased cortical thickness. *NeuroReport* 16:1893–1897.

Leary, M. R., C. E. Adams, and E. B. Tate. 2006. Hypo-egoic self-regulation: Exercising self-control by diminishing the influence of the self. *Journal of Personality* 74:180–183.

Leary, M. R., and N. R. Buttermore. 2003. The evolution of the human self: Tracing the natural history of self-awareness. *Journal for the Theory of Social Behaviour* 33:365–404.

Leary, M., E. Tate, C. Adams, A. Allen, and J. Hancock. 2007. Self-compassion and reactions to unpleasant self-relevant events: The implications of treating oneself kindly. *Journal of Personality* 92:887–904.

LeDoux, J. E. 1995. Emotion: Clues from the brain. *Annual Review of Psychology* 46:209–235.

———. 2003. *Synaptic Self: How Our Brains Become Who We Are.* New York: Penguin.

Legrand, D. and Ruby, P. 2009. What is self-specific? Theoretical investigation and critical review of neuroimaging results. *Psychological Review* 116: 252–282.

Lewis, M. D. 2005. Self-organizing individual differences in brain development. *Developmental Review* 25:252–277.

Lewis, M. D., and R. M. Todd. 2007. The self-regulating brain: Cortical-subcortical feedback and the development of intelligent action. *Cognitive Development* 22:406–430.

Libet, B. 1999. Do we have free will? *Journal of Consciousness Studies* 6:47–57.

Licinio J., P. W. Gold, and M. L. Wong. 1995. A molecular mechanism for stress-induced alterations in susceptibility to disease. *Lancet* 346:104–106.

Lieberman, M., N. Eisenberg, M. Crocket, S. Tom, J. Pfeifer, and B. Way. 2007. Putting feelings into words. *Psychological Science* 18:421–428.

Lilly, J. 2006. *The Deep Self: Consciousness Exploration in the Isolation Tank.* Nevada City, CA: Gateways Books and Tapes.

Linden, D. J. 2007. *The Accidental Mind: How Brain Evolution Has Given Us Love, Memory, Dreams, and God.* Cambridge, MA: The Belknap Press of Harvard University Press.

Luders, E., A. W. Toga, N. Lepore, and C. Gaser. 2009. The underlying anatomical correlates of long-term meditation: larger hippocampal and frontal volumes of gray matter. *Neuroimage* 45:672–678.

Luskin, F., M. Reitz, K. Newell, T. G. Quinn, and W. Haskell. 2002. A controlled pilot study of stress management training of elderly patients with congestive heart failure. *Preventive Cardiology* 5:168–174.

Lutz, A., J. Brefczynski-Lewis, T. Johnstone, and R. Davidson. 2008. Regulation of the neural circuitry of emotion by compassion meditation: Effects of meditative expertise. *PLoS ONE* 3(3):e1897.

Lutz, A., L. Greischar, N. Rawlings, M. Ricard, and R. Davidson. 2004. Long-term meditators self-induce high-amplitude gamma synchrony during mental practice. *Proceedings of the National Academy of Sciences* 101:16369–16373.

Lutz, A., J. Lachaux, J. Martinerie, and F. Varela. 2002. Guiding the study of brain dynamics by first-person data: Synchrony patterns correlate with ongoing conscious states during a simple visual task. *Proceedings of the National Academy of Sciences* 99:1586–1591.

Lutz, A., H. A. Slager, J. D. Dunne, and R. J. Davidson. 2008. Attention regulation and monitoring in meditation. *Trends in Cognitive Sciences* 12:163–169.

Ma, Q. L., B. Teter, O. J. Ubeda, T. Morihara, D. Dhoot, M. D. Nyby, M. L. Tuck, S. A. Frautschy, and G. M. Cole. 2007. Omega-3 fatty acid docosahexaenoic acid increases SorLA/LR11, a sorting protein with reduced expression in sporadic Alzheimer's disease (AD): Relevance to AD prevention. *The Journal of Neuroscience* 27:14299–14307.

Mackenzie, M. 2009. Enacting the self: Buddhist and Enactivist approaches to the emergence of the self. *Phenomenology and the Cognitive Sciences* (in press).

MacLean, P. D. 1990. *The Triune Brain in Evolution: Role in Paleocerebral Functions*. New York: Springer.

Maguire, E., D. Gadian, I. Johnsrude, C. Good, J. Ashburner, R. Frackowiak, and C. Frith. 2000. Navigation-related structural change in the hippocampi of taxi drivers. *Proceedings of the National Academy of Sciences* 97:4398–4403.

Main, M., E. Hesse, and N. Kaplan. 2005. Predictability of attachment behavior and representational processes at 1, 6, and 19 years of age: The Berkeley Longitudinal Study. In *Attachment from Infancy to Adulthood: The Major Longitudinal Studies*, edited by K. E. Grossmann, K. Grossmann, and E. Waters. New York: Guilford Press.

Maletic, V., M. Robinson, T. Oakes, S. Iyengar, S. G. Ball, and J. Russell. 2007. Neurobiology of Depression: An Integrated View Of Key Findings. *International Journal of Clinical Practice* 61:2030–2040.

Marz, R. B. 1999. *Medical Nutrition from Marz*, 2nd ed. Portland OR: Omni Press.

McClure, S. M., D. I. Laibson, G. Loewenstein, and J. D. Cohen. 2004. Separate neural systems value immediate and delayed monetary rewards. *Science* 306:503–507.

McCraty, R., M. Atkinson, and D. Thomasino. 2003. Impact of a workplace stress reduction program on blood pressure and emotional health in hypertensive employees. *Journal of Alternative and Complementary Medicine* 9:355–369.

Messier, C., and M. Gagnon. 2000. Glucose regulation and brain aging: Nutrition and cognitive decline. *The Journal of Nutrition, Health, and Aging* 4:208–213.

Meyer, J. S., and L. F. Quenzer. 2004. *Psychopharmacology: Drugs, the Brain, and Behavior.* Sunderland, MA: Sinauer Associates.

Miller, A. 2008. The methylation, neurotransmitter, and antioxidant connections between folate and depression. *Alternative Medicine Review* 13(3):216–226.

Moll, J., F. Krueger, R. Zahn, M. Pardini, R. Oliveira-Souza, and J. Grafman. 2006. Human fronto-mesolimbic networks guide decisions about charitable donation. *Proceedings of the National Academy of Sciences* 103:15623–15628.

Monfils, M-H., K. K. Cowansage, E. Klann, and J. LeDoux. 2002. Extinction-reconsolidation boundaries: Key to persistent attenuation of fear memories. *Science* 324:951–955.

Morris, M. C., D. A. Evans, C. C. Tangney, J. L. Bienias, R. S. Wilson, N. T. Aggarwal, and P. A. Scherr. 2005. Relation of the tocopherol forms to incident Alzheimer disease and to cognitive change. *American Journal of Clinical Nutrition* 81:508–514.

Murray, R. K., D. K. Granner, P. A. Mayes, and V. W. Rodwell. 2000. *Harper's Biochemistry*, 25th ed. New York: McGraw-Hill.

Nanamoli, B. and B. Bodhi. 1995. *The Middle Length Discourses of the Buddha: A Translation of the Majjhima Nikaya (Teachings of the Buddha).* Boston: Wisdom Publications.

Niedenthal, P. 2007. Embodying emotion. *Science* 316:1002.

Nimchinsky, E., E. Gilissen, J. Allman, D. Perl, J. Erwin, and P. Hof. 1999. A neuronal morphologic type unique to humans and great apes. *Proceedings of the National Academy of Science* 96:5268–5273.

Norenzayan, A. and A. F. Shariff. 2008. The origin and evolution of religious prosociality. *Science* 322:58–62.

Nowak, M. 2006. Five rules for the evolution of cooperation. *Science* 314:1560–1563.

Oberman, L. M., and V. S. Ramachandran. 2007. The simulating social mind: The role of the mirror neuron system and simulation in the social and communicative deficits of autism spectrum disorders. *Psychology Bulletin* 133:310–327.

O'Reilly, R. 2006. Biologically based computational models of high-level cognition. *Science* 314:91–94.

Pare, D., D. R. Collins, and J. G. Pelletier. 2002. Amygdala oscillations and the consolidation of emotional memories. *Trends in Cognitive Sciences* 6:306–314.

Park, M., G. W. Ross, H. Petrovitch, L. R. White, K. H. Masaki, J. S. Nelson, C. M. Tanner, J. D. Curb, P. L. Blanchette, and R. D. Abbott. 2005. Consumption of milk and calcium in midlife and the future risk of Parkinson disease. *Neurology* 64:1047–1051.

Paus, T. 2001. Primate anterior cingulate cortex: Where motor control, drive, and cognition interface. *Nature Reviews Neuroscience* 2:417–424.

Pedata, F., L. Giovannelli, G. Spignoli, M. G. Giovannini, and G. Pepeu. 1985. Phosphatidylserine increases acetylcholine release from cortical slices in aged rats. *Neurobiology of Aging* 6:337–339.

Peeters, G. and J. Czapinski. 1990. Positive-negative asymmetry in evaluations: The distinction between affective and informational negativity effects. In *European Review of Social Psychology: Volume 1*, edited by W. Stroebe and M. Hewstone. New York: Wiley.

Petrovic, P., R. Kalisch, T. Singer, and R. J. Dolan. 2008. Oxytocin attenuates affective evaluations of conditioned faces and amygdala activity. *Journal of Neuroscience* 28:6607–6615.

Pitcher, D., L. Garrido, V. Walsh, and B. C. Duchaine. 2008. Transcranial magnetic stimulation disrupts the perception and embodiment of facial expressions. *The Journal of Neuroscience* 28:8929–8933.

Posner, M. I., and M. K. Rothbart. 2000. Developing mechanisms of self-regulation. *Development and Psychopathology* 12:427–441.

Puri, B. K. 2006. High-resolution magnetic resonance imaging sinc-interpolation-based subvoxel registration and semi-automated quantitative lateral ventricular morphology employing threshold computation and binary image creation in the study of fatty acid interventions in schizophrenia, depression, chronic fatigue syndrome, and Huntington's disease. *International Review of Psychiatry* 18:149–154.

Quirk, G. J., J. C. Repa, and J. E. LeDoux. 1995. Fear conditioning enhances short-latency auditory responses of lateral amygdala neurons: Parallel recordings in the freely behaving rat. *Neuron* 15:1029–1039.

Rabinovich, M., R. Huerta, and G. Laurent. 2008. Transient dynamics for neural processing. *Science* 321:48–50.

Raichle, M. 2006. The brain's dark energy. *Science* 314:1249–1250.

Raichle, M., and D. Gusnard. 2002. Appraising the brain's energy budget. *Proceedings of the National Academy of Sciences* 99:10237–10239.

Raichle, M. E., A. M. MacLeod, A. Z. Snyder, W. J. Powers, D. A. Gusnard, and G. L. Shumlan. 2001. A default mode of brain function. *Proceedings of the National Academy of Sciences* 98:676–682.

Rasia-Filho, A., R. Londero, and M. Achaval. 2000. Functional activities of the amygdala: An overview. *Journal of Psychiatry and Neuroscience* 25:14–23.

Rilling, J., D. Gutman, T. Zeh, G. Pagnoni, G. Berns, and C. Kilts. 2002. A neural basis for social cooperation. *Neuron* 35:395–405.

Robinson, P. 2007. How to fill a synapse. *Science* 316:551–553.

Rosenberg, M. 2008 Second Edition. *Nonviolent Communication: A Language of Life*. Chicago: Puddledancer Press.

Sapolsky, R. M. 1998. *Why Zebras Don't Get Ulcers*. New York: W. H. Freeman Co.

———. 2006. A natural history of peace. *Foreign Affairs* 85:104-121.

Schechner, S. 2008. Keeping love alive. *Wall Street Journal*, February 8, W1.

Schore, A. 2003. *Affect Regulation and the Repair of the Self.* New York: W. W. Norton.

Seligman, M. 2006. *Learned Optimism: How to Change Your Mind and Your Life*. New York: Vintage/Random House.

Semaw, S., S. Renne, J. W. K. Harris, C. S. Feibel, R. L. Bernor, N. Fesseha, and K. Mowbray. 1997. 2.5-million-year-old stone tools from Gona, Ethiopia. *Nature* 385:333–336.

Shantideva. 1997. *The Way of the Bodhisattva: A Translation of the Bodhicharyavatara*. Boston: Shambhala.

Shutt, K., A. MacLarnon, M. Heistermann, and S. Semple. 2007. Grooming in Barbary macaques: Better to give than to receive? *Biology Letters* 3:231–233.

Siegel, D. J. 2001. *The Developing Mind*. New York: Guilford Press.

———. 2007. *The Mindful Brain: Reflection and Attunement in the Cultivation of Well-Being*. New York: W. W. Norton and Co.

Silk, J. B. 2007. Social components of fitness in primate groups. *Science* 317:1347–1351.

Simpson, S. W., J. Quade, N. E. Levin, R. Butler, G. Dupont-Nivet, M. Everett, and S. Semaw. 2008. A female *Homo erectus* pelvis from Gona, Ethiopia. *Science* 322:1089–1092.

Singer, T. 2006. The neuronal basis and ontogeny of empathy and mind reading. *Neuroscience and Biobehavioral Reviews* 30:855–863.

Singer, T., B. Seymour, J. O'Doherty, H. Kaube, R. J. Dolan, and C. D. Frith. 2004. Empathy for pain involves the affective but not sensory components of pain. *Science* 303:1157–1162.

Singer, T., B. Seymour, J. O'Doherty, K. Stephan, R. Dolan, and C. Frith. 2006. Empathic neural responses are modulated by the perceived fairness of others. *Nature* 439:466–469.

Singh, M. 2005. Essential fatty acids, DHA, and human brain. *Indian Journal of Pediatrics* 72:239–242.

Spagnoli, A., U. Lucca, G. Menasce, L. Bandera, G. Cizza, G. Forloni, M. Tettamanti, L. Frattura, P. Tiraboschi, M. Comelli, U. Senin, A. Longo, A. Petrini, G. Brambilla, A. Belloni, C. Negri, F. Cavazzuti, A. Salsi, P. Calogero, E. Parma, M. Stramba-Badiale, S. Vitali, G. Andreoni, M. R. Inzoli, G. Santus, R. Caregnato, M. Peruzza, M. Favaretto, C. Bozeglav, M. Alberoni, D. de Leo, L. Serraiotto, A. Baiocchi, S. Scoccia, P. Culotta, and D. Ieracitano. 1991. Long-term acetyl-L-carnitine treatment in Alzheimer's disease. *Neurology* 41:1726.

Spear, L. P., 2000. The adolescent brain and age-related behavioral manifestations. *Neuroscience Biobehavior Review* 24:417–463.

Stern, D. 2000. *The Interpersonal World of the Infant.* New York: Basic Books.

Su, K., S. Huang, C. Chiub, and W. Shenc. 2003. Omega-3 fatty acids in major depressive disorder: A preliminary double-blind, placebo-controlled trial. *European Neuropsychopharmacology* 13:267–271.

Sumedho, A. 2006. Trust in awareness. Talk given at Chithurst Monastery, Chithurst, UK, February 25.

Sun, Q. Q., S. S. Xu, J. L. Pan, H. M. Guo, and W. Q. Cao. 1999. Huperzine-A capsules enhance memory and learning performance in 34 pairs of matched adolescent students. *Zhongguo yao li xue bao [Acta Pharmacologica Sinica]* 20:601–603.

Takahashi, H., M. Kato, M. Matsuura, D. Mobbs, T. Suhara, and Y. Okubo. 2009. When your gain is my pain and your pain is my gain: Neural correlates of envy and schadenfreude. *Science* 323:937–939.

Tanaka, J., Y. Horiike, M. Matsuzaki, T. Miyazka, G. Ellis-David, and H. Kasai. 2008. Protein synthesis and neurotrophin-dependent structural plasticity of single dendritic spines. *Science* 319:1683–1687.

Tang, Y., Y. Ma, J. Wang, Y. Fan, S. Feg, Q. Lu, Q. Yu, D. Sui, M. Rothbart, M. Fan, and M. Posner. 2007. Short-term meditation training improves attention and self-regulation. *Proceedings of the National Academy of Sciences* 104:17152–17156.

Taylor, S. E., L. C. Klein, B. P. Lewis, T. L. Gruenewald, R. A. R. Gurung, and J. A. Updegraff. 2000. Biobehavioral responses to stress in females: Tend-and-befriend, not fight-or-flight. *Psychological Review* 107:411–429.

Thera, N. 1993. The four sublime states: Contemplations on love, compassion, sympathetic joy, and equanimity. Retrieved from http://www.accesstoinsight.org/lib/authors/nyanaponika/wheel006.html on April 3, 2009.

Thompson, E. 2007. *Mind in Life: Biology, Phenomenology, and the Sciences of Mind.* Cambridge, MA: Harvard University Press.

Thompson, E., and F. J. Varela. 2001. Radical embodiment: Neural dynamics and consciousness. *Trends in Cognitive Sciences* 5:418–425.

Tucker, D. M., D. Derryberry, and P. Luu. 2000. Anatomy and physiology of human emotion: Vertical integration of brain stem, limbic, and cortical systems. In *Handbook of the Neuropsychology of Emotion*, edited by J. Borod. London: Oxford University Press.

Vaish, A., T. Grossmann, and A. Woodward. 2008. Not all emotions are created equal: The negativity bias in social-emotional development. *Psychological Bulletin* 134:383–403.

Vaitl, D., J. Gruzelier, G. Jamieson, D. Lehmann, U. Ott, G. Sammer, U. Strehl, N. Birbaumer, B. Kotchoubey, A. Kubler, W. Miltner, P. Putz, I. Strauch, J. Wackermann, and T. Weiss. 2005. Psychobiology of altered states of consciousness. *Psychological Bulletin* 133:149–182.

Vogiatzoglou, A., H. Refsum, C. Johnston, S. M. Smith, K. M. Bradley, C. de Jager, M. M. Budge, and A. D. Smith, 2008. Vitamin B12 status and rate of brain volume loss in community-dwelling elderly. *Neurology* 71:826–832.

Walsh, R., and S. L. Shapiro. 2006. The meeting of meditative disciplines and Western psychology: A mutually enriching dialogue. *American Psychologist* 61:227–239.

Wilson, E. O. 1999. *Consilience: The Unity of Knowledge.* London: Random House/Vintage Books.

Wolf, J. L. 1995. Bowel function. In *Primary Care of Women*, edited by K. J. Carlson and S. A. Eisenstat. St. Louis, MO: Mosby-Year Book, Inc.

Wu, W., A. M. Brickman, J. Luchsinger, P. Ferrazzano, P. Pichiule, M. Yoshita, T. Brown, C. DeCarli, C. A. Barnes, R. Mayeux, S. Vannucci, and S. A. Small. 2008. The brain in the age of old: The hippocampal formation is targeted differentially by diseases of late life. *Annals of Neurology* 64:698–706.

Yamasaki, H., K. LaBar, and G. McCarthy. 2002. Dissociable prefrontal brain systems for attention and emotion. *Proceedings of the National Academy of Sciences* 99:11447–11451.

Yang, E., D. Zald, and R. Blake. 2007. Fearful expressions gain preferential access to awareness during continuous flash suppression. *Emotion* 7:882–886.

Young, L., and Z. Wang. 2004. The neurobiology of pair bonding. *Nature Neuroscience* 7:1048–1054.

Zelazo, P. D., H. H. Gao, and R. Todd. 2003. The development of consciousness. In *The Cambridge Handbook of Consciousness*, edited by P. D. Zelazo, M. Moscovitch, and E. Thompson. New York: Cambridge University Press.

Rick Hanson, Ph.D., is a neuropsychologist and meditation teacher. A *summa cum laude* graduate of the University of California, Los Angeles, he cofounded the Wellspring Institute for Neuroscience and Contemplative Wisdom and edits the Wise Brain Bulletin. He and his wife have two children.

Richard Mendius, MD, is a neurologist and cofounder of the Wellspring Institute for Neuroscience and Contemplative Wisdom. He has taught medicine at University of California, Los Angeles, and Stanford University in Palo Alto, CA. He also teaches weekly meditation classes at San Quentin State Prison. He and his wife have three children.

Foreword writer **Daniel J. Siegel, MD**, is executive director of the Mindsight Institute and an associate clinical professor of psychiatry in the School of Medicine at the University of California, Los Angeles. He is author of *The Developing Mind*, *The Mindful Brain*, and other books, and is founding editor of the Norton Series on Interpersonal Neurobiology.

Preface writer **Jack Kornfield, Ph.D.**, is cofounder of the Insight Meditation Society in Barre, MA, and a founding teacher of Spirit Rock Meditation Center in Woodacre, CA. He is author of many books, including *A Path with Heart* and *The Wise Heart*.

Discover the Simple Method to More Joy and Less Stress

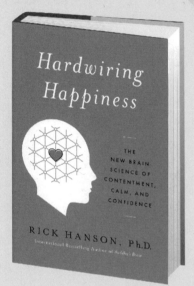

"This book offers simple, accessible, practical steps for touching the peace and joy that are every person's birthright."
—Thich Nhat Hanh, author of *Being Peace* and *Understanding Our Mind*

"Rick Hanson is a master of his craft, showing us a wise path for daily living. Here is a book to savor, to practice, and to take to heart."
—Mark Williams, Ph.D., Professor, University of Oxford, author of *Mindfulness*